DESPAIR AND MODERNITY

Despair and Modernity

Reflections from Modern Indian Painting

HARSHA V. DEHEJIA

with

PREM SHANKAR JHA AND RANJIT HOSKOTE

with a Foreword by

ASHIS NANDY

MOTILAL BANARSIDASS PUBLISHERS
PRIVATE LIMITED • DELHI

First Edition: Delhi, 2000

ISBN: 81-208-1755-9

Also available at:

MOTILAL BANARSIDASS

236, 9th Main III Block, Jayanagar, Bangalore 560 011
41 U.A. Bungalow Road, Jawahar Nagar, Delhi 110 007
8 Mahalaxmi Chamber, Warden Road, Mumbai 400 026
120 Royapettah High Road, Mylapore, Chennai 600 004
Sanas Plaza, 1302 Baji Rao Road, Pune 411 002
8 Camac Street, Calcutta 700 017
Ashok Rajpath, Patna 800 004
Chowk, Varanasi 221 001

Printed in India

BY JAINENDRA PRAKASH JAIN AT SHRI JAINENDRA PRESS,
A-45 NARAINA, PHASE-I, NEW DELHI 110 028
AND PUBLISHED BY NARENDRA PRAKASH JAIN FOR
MOTILAL BANARSIDASS PUBLISHERS PRIVATE LIMITED,
BUNGALOW ROAD, DELHI 110 007

for
Vivek
who has shown us the beauty of urban spaces
and Rajeev
who fills spaces in our lives
with beautiful words

FOREWORD

Ashis Nandy

The classical forms of creativity and philosophy of arts in India do not have any recognized place for three states of consciousness: despair, banality and absurdity. Indian classicism, however, does have a place for sorrow, cynicism, pessimism, and even self-alienation. It has also a place for, as anyone who has read Bhāsa will know, the trivial, the low brow and the comic. But, till now it has shown no sign of formally registering a state of despair, an emotion that afflicts, for instance, some works of Van Gogh or Franz Kafka, involving a sense of the futility of it all, melancholia or total hopelessness. Nor have they created a place for the cultivated pop that celebrates the banal the way Andy Wharhol does or for the unashamedly surreal. Of the three states, this book is concerned with the first, as it affects aesthetic philosophy and awareness.

The absence of a proper philosophical and aesthetic status for despair is not unique to Indian traditions. Despair is alien to most traditional cultures, including pre-modern Europe. True, some have mentioned the personification of despair in Judas Iscariot in Late Antiquity Europe. His betrayal of Christ and subsequent suicide, it has been argued, have left their mark on European consciousness. Surely, one sees the shadow of that Biblical instance of desperation and self-destruction in modern times on the likes of Friedrich Nietzsche, when he takes on the voice of a madman to proclaim that God is dead and that we are the ones to have killed him. However, it is doubtful if that pre-modern model of despair has any close philosophical links with the full blown recognition of ontological despair in our times that Nietzsche himself comes close to admitting. One is tempted to affirm that, in pre-modern West, despair as a philosophy of art or of literature was not known. The most one can say is that some works of art and some characters in literature, Sophocles' *Oedipus* and Shakespeare's *King Lear*, for instance, can be read as pointers to, rather than instances of an ontology of despair. Perhaps, despair traditionally is not so much an unknown state of mind as a rare analytic category. It is an existential state that has acquired a serious moral, philosophical and aesthetic status only in modern times.

It can be argued that in South Asian traditions one guesses that even when confronted with total existential hopelessness, in a world imbued with sacredness and alive with transcendental possibilities, existential hopelessness does not easily translate into the hopelessness of the soul. In these ancient civilizations despair remains a psycho-social response rather than a philosophical position. I use the term 'transcendental' broadly here, not necessarily in the sense in which it has been used at places in this book. In Mahābhārata, after Kṛṣṇa reveals to Karna the secret of his birth, Karna has every reason to give in to despair, but he does not. Both life and death continue to make sense to him, as does the difference between them. Even in contemporary Europe the open-ended, fuzzy transcendentalism in the world-view of Albert Einstein and Arther Schroedinger supplies, in the form of a unified or integrated philosophy or meaningful frame of life, a defense against an utter hopelessness that infects the creative efforts of many like Samuel Beckett. Even when his world-view comes close to the idea of despair, Albert Camus remains somewhere in touch with hope, unlike Van Gogh. Indeed, Camus imposes a framework on an existential experience that recognizes the first or primordial question: why should I not commit suicide? He answers it by imposing a meaning on his world by a sheer act of will.

On the whole, however, a philosophy of despair has more immediate relevance and appeal in secularized and urban societies where the individual has been atomized and cut off from most community ties and where impersonal, contractual relationships have come to dominate social life. For, everything said, for despair to be something more than an artistic posture, the gods have to die. Harsha Dehejia's term for despair, *nāstika nairāśya*, makes that clear. Even existential despair is primarily the disease of a society, that offers its inhabitants not merely the option of a nihilistic world-view, but also fragments a way of life that contributes to or underwrites the nihilism, and the tacit, if sectional, codes of conduct that legitimize it. However, it is doubtful if even the term *nāstik nairāśya* captures for the older South Asian philosophies of art, the range of meanings associated with the concept of despair. This book itself recognizes that atheism enjoys a certain legitimacy in the Indian spiritual domain that Nietzsche could not have dreamt of. In Buddhism, Jainism and in philosophical schools represented by the likes of Cārvāka, for instance, atheism, godlessness or the denial of the authority of the Vedas does not convey the feeling of total abandonment and hopelessness, tinged with a touch of rebelliousness, that it does in European Judeo-Christian traditions. South Asian atheism certainly does not convey any impassioned acknowledgment of utter loneliness in a godless universe, that forces one to define one's own fate, morality and meaning of life. However, things have been changing in South Asia during the last hundred and fifty years.

The reasonably stable psycho-ecological balance, which large sections of people have experienced in the region for centuries is now under severe stress. First of all, the introduction of modern political economy under an apathetic colonial regime and the gradual spread of values and systems of knowledge, inadequately sensitive to the cultural, environmental and community-based concerns of the region, have been traumatic. The breakdown of embedded theories of life that once mediated between the sacred and the profane and above all, the introduction of a ruthless theory of progress and its cannibalistic progeny developmentalism, have released cultural forces that threaten to destroy that balance. Not so much by subverting a pan-Indian way of life, as Prem Shankar Jha in his essay seems to suggest, as by subverting and desacralising the diverse integrated concepts of life. Jha's argument has, however, a hidden dimension of which he seems unaware. Many of the communities now facing despair are exactly the ones that have lived with world views that are more integrated and do not allow the controlled splits with which the Brahminic world view is more at ease. What was once a source of strength has thus become a source of vulnerability. Between them, the breakdown and uncritical progressivism have turned despair into a recognizable state of mind in the landscape of Indian creativity. Despair is not incomprehensible in Indian arts and letters any more; it hounds many painters, writers and thinkers. Despair has become an unwelcome house guest who shows no sign of cutting short its stay.

Dehejia has tried to create a place within the main frame of culture and philosophy of Indian art for a legitimate analytic theory called despair. Till recently, art criticism in India kept double ledgers. There have been aesthetic theories of the pre-modern and the folk, and there have been aesthetic theories of the modern. Dehejia's effort creates a space for the modern within Indian classicism, by negotiating the philosophy of despair in classical terms. As a result the basic schism that has grown in recent years between the philosophy and history of modern art, on the one hand and the philosophy and history of traditional arts, is today closer to being breached. This is no mean achievement.

Perhaps because of the emphasis on individual artists in the following essays, in Dehejia's over all scheme of things, there is no place for despair of communities. There is also an open admission in this book that it takes the approach of an antiquarian to reconstruct a civilization by concentrating on the arts. Such an approach by-passes the verbal testimony of those living in or with the civilization. Yet life has a way of gate crashing into the arts that aesthetic theories in no age are ever able to handle. This is mainly because the translation from the passions of life to the passions of art is neither perfect nor entirely transparent. One can even argue, using some of the same sources that Dehejia uses in this book, that art in any society can be a double edged weapon. It can be both a creatively distorted reflection and a defensive shield against changing civilizational realities. The double edged nature of art is patent in contemporary South Asia where commentaries on arts have become more distant from the carriers of art and their cosmological crises.

I foresee a time when the entire Indian tradition of artisans and craftsmen and women and the communities that have come to represent these traditions will begin to move quickly towards a state of massive epidemic of despair. Probably they are already doing so. This epidemic cannot be interpreted as only a matter of individual choice or individual psychopathology. Nor can we wait for a creative response to this despair to emerge from the artistic products of the communities, for these forms of artistic self-expression are themselves threatened by the new social and cultural forces unleashed in the region. The sudden spurt of suicides among the farmers of Andhra Pradesh, Maharashtra and Karnataka in 1998, which spread like a contagious disease is a grim pointer to the way things might move in the future. The most important point to remember in connection with these suicides was that the desperation of the farmers was not an individual character trait that afflicted lonely, isolated, desperate individuals as in classical instances of despair in the modern West.

The Indian farmers did not commit suicide the way some businessmen did in the 1930s, during the great depression in the United States. Even in their desperation, these Indian farmers retained some tenuous grip on life affirmative forces. For instance, many of them hoped that the compensation the family would get on their death would itself mitigate the suffering of their family. Their self-destruction often came packaged in a self-designed, calculated self-sacrifice. To that extent, they remained, even in their death, just outside the rim of true despair and the self-destruction that comes from the amalgam of utter hopelessness and total meaninglessness of life. Their suicide was not merely a response to the existential question: why should we not commit suicide? It was often a response to a question that had a very different philosophical tone to it: are we not more useful to the world dead than living?

The fate of south Indian farmers should have made us aware that despair in India might now stalk entire communities, the way it has done in the case of a number of American Indian communities that Kai Erikson describes in his book *A New Species of Trouble.* One-third of all Indian tribes, Smitu Kothari tells us, have already been totally uprooted from their traditional habitat by the process of development. They have become parts of flotsam and jetsam that have surfaced in India's urban slums, in the wake of South Asia's march towards development and, now, globalized capitalism.

The four crucial, if tacit concepts that frame South Asian culture of public life today are obsolescence, dispensability, exile and invisibility of sizeable parts of the Indian population. We have unilaterally declared that, according to the latest available textbooks of social change that in the name of progress and development, entire communities, lifestyles, tribes and systems of knowledge associated with them have become redundant. When we talk of them or their cultural assets and traditional knowledge, we usually do so in the past tense. Indeed, we talk of them as if they lived in some distant past, romanticized by impractical visionaries such as M. K. Gandhi, Rabindranath Tagore, J. C. Kumarappa and Ananda Coomaraswamy or politicized by obstreperous, self-serving activists, such as Medha Patkar, Sundarlal Bahuguna and Vandana Shiva.

Even much of the rhetoric of population control in the region is a response to the shared anxiety in middle class India that the obsolete and the redundant continue to be a drain on the resources of the country. There is a growing consensus that enlightened democratic regimes should facilitate, if not actually do what some of the colonial regimes did in the Southern world to the native populations in Africa and the Americas, and allow them to gracefully slide into oblivion in glorified reservations or sanctuaries. There is of course the other exit policy that wishes that communities and persons unable to adjust to the current concepts of the new and the progressive should not, ideally, strain the resources of a poor country and graciously waste themselves for the sake of their compatriots. Most of the times, the affected populations are not even visible to us; and they know that they are merely statistics, open for public inspection and subject to academic debate. This desperation threatens to make the despair in many urban Indian artists, writers and thinkers look feigned or artificial even when perfectly genuine.

Organized social knowledge might have avoided them, but the four tacit concepts: obsolescence, dispensability, exile and invisibility, will have to explicitly constitute, I suspect, the core of any future social knowledge that hopes to meet the ethical test of our times. Dehejia's openness to the idea of despair, reflecting the openness of the classical Indian philosophy of art, will also mean a new sensitivity to the sources of despair in the contemporary world. These sources are usually manufactured, though it remains an open question if the process of social change that have brought them about are themselves reversible.

This is doubly important because creativity, both as an activity and as a state of mind, must use a new chemistry of existing emotions, motives and fantasies of creativity. Neither can it start from scratch, nor can it use the available chemistry as a given. An encumbered mind is rarely creative. If some creative artists and writers feel that they have a right to despair and give vent to their despair, we shall have to take that urge seriously. For it allows us to connect to the empirics of despair outside us. For artists and writers in toying with or playfully exploring the idea of despair are often authentic by default. We must seriously consider their sources of creativity, whether we like them or not, whether they are reasonable or not. This means that if Indian traditions do not have a category that describes contemporary feelings of despair, such categories will have to be produced from within the Indian aesthetic experience, theory and philosophy. For that is the only way one can link the experience of the many to the creativity of a few.

It is that story that Harsha Dehejia and his associates try to tell in this book through the canvas of contemporary Indian paintings. True to the Indian traditions of art, the writers, particularly Dehejia, do not shy away from the philosophy of art and do not concentrate on only art history and aesthetic theory when he confronts the experience of despair, either as a motivating chemistry in Indian arts or as an ontological position. Indeed, they seek to locate the experience in the Indian philosophy of art. This is only appropriate, for when centuries ago Indian aesthetics internalized the concept of *śānta* rasa, not merely changing experience and moral vision but Buddhist philosophy mediated that innovation.

It seems to emerge from these papers that there are two major sources of despair in contemporary Indian creativity: the subversion of the self by colonialism in various spheres of life and the wholesale substitution of the non-rational and the mythic by the rational and the realistic. These developments are not fully independent of each other, for the subversion of the self was undertaken in the name of rationality and realism, and the persistence of the non-rational and the mythic was as a justification of the colonial theory of civilizational mission. The new political economy that began to destroy the life support system of many South Asian communities in the nineteenth century was seen to enjoy the patronage of the irreversible processes of scientific growth and social progress. Old societies are frequently activated by radical challenges and both these sources of despair might have also opened up new possibilities in Indian art and literature, even if by underwriting the spread of despair as a psycho-social and philosophical state. Existing works on despair know neither of the two categories, though it might be able to accommodate the former within its framework more easily than the latter. Self-alienation is known in the West, though self-alienation induced though cultural engineering may not be. More difficult to reconcile with contemporary aesthetic theory and art criticism could be the second source of despair in Indian arts, namely the displacement of the non-rational by the rational and the mythic by the historical. Even those uncomfortable with the presumptions of social evolutionism will consider the displacements as a natural and necessary correction of Indian society and part of an inevitable process of global change. Indeed, contemporary commonsense seems to assume that the movement from the non-rational and the mythic to the rational and the historical is the clue to the emergence of philosophy.

The end result is that, along with homelessness, breakdown of some of the central social institutions, cynicism and pessimism, there has spread a philosophical pessimism hitched to an increasingly nihilistic world image. Contemporary Indian creativity has begun to speak of, or represent, what to a growing number of Indians looks like the utter hopelessness of the human condition itself. For this at least there was no precedence in the older world views of India, classical or folk, high cultural or low, Brahminic or non-Brahminic, Hindu or non-Hindu.

As it happens, this renegotiated status of despair in Indian theories of art links up in a strange way with the melancholia of what could be called post-Enlightenment modernity. When gods die, they leave behind the ruins of a moral order and a fragile and transient set of aesthetic and ethical values that defy all hierarchies and priorities. As a result, the high culture of modernity is now partly defined by its inverse, a sustained radical critique of modernity and the overall tone of our times can now be summed up in that overworked expression, 'modernity as loss'. Even with regard to the operative philosophy of modernity there seems to have appeared a cleavage and a hierarchy of cultures. Those living with the advanced versions of modernity live with its more nuanced, slightly self-deprecating form. Post-modernism is basically a derivation from that. The apprentice societies trying to catch up, whether in Asia or East Europe are expected to act as drummer boys of modernity's nineteenth century colonial version. By locating the experience of despair within the Indian philosophy of art one also makes the riches of that philosophy available for understanding a state of mind now inextricably intertwined with the experience of contemporary artistic creativity. Scholars, activists and observers of the Indian life and contemporary arts will be grateful to Harsha Dehejia, Prem Shankar Jha and Ranjit Hoskote for the scope and innovativeness of their venture.

CONTENTS

1
INTRODUCTION

Harsha V. Dehejia

To someone steeped in our ancient art and aesthetic traditions the first serious encounter with modern Indian art becomes not only problematic but a bit bewildering. One discovers that in the world of modern art, the mythic beings of ancient art have given way to mortals, the ordered universe as prescribed in the *śilpaśāstras* is nowhere to be found, Bharata's injunctions about *rasa* seem to be ignored, the traditional dictates of ancient Tamil and Sanskrit poetry have been abandoned, the well worn symbols of the tradition are replaced by a private artistic language and the world of anonymity of the sage artist has changed to a cult of personalities of modern artists. One reaction of the traditional *rasika* is to retreat into the safety of a Chola bronze or the comfort of a Pahadi miniature, the aura of the loving images of Khajuraho or the charm of an illuminated manuscript. For to be with ancient art is like being with elders, where one feels a sense of serenity and continuity, where the world appears ordered, where one can live in the present and yet not have to give up treasured memories of the past, where conversation is replete with mythic metaphors, where Kalidasa flows as easily as Jayadeva. To be with ancient and traditional art is to feel secure and restful, to experience a certain *pūrṇatva*, completeness, and not fragmentation, to be drawn to the still centre of the universe rather than be scattered.

But what about the plethora of modern art that surrounds us, the many art galleries that summon us, where the creative output of our modern artists wait in muted voices waiting to be heard or the museums of modern art where one enters with some trepidation? Are we to turn our back on this new and important chapter of Indian art, not pay it serious attention and dismiss it as something beyond our comprehension? Are we to fall prey to the pedestrian and subjective tendency of calling it just good or bad, or treat it as mere decoration or worse still to evaluate it on a rupee per square inch basis?

A deep, contemplative, serious and aesthetic celebration of any art form requires that it be done through establishing first and foremost its *artha*, meaning. It is an accepted aesthetic doctrine that unless a piece of art is semantically driven it will remain a mere decoration and provide only superficial enjoyment rather than a meaningful aesthetic experience. To a serious aesthete and to a committed student of art, art therefore must be contemplatively understood, its symbols decoded in tranquillity and its layers of meanings established, enjoyed and experienced to the fullest, so that art experience becomes a chastening experience rather than a trivial art encounter. To be distracted by the persona of the artist, journalistic art criticisms, social or psychological factors associated with the artist or the art object or by the market value of that art is to engage in superficial, unaesthetic and unproductive activities. We must take our stand on the art object and then proceed to discourse about it, leaving behind the artist, the art critic and the art dealer. The art object must stand on its own for our serious consideration.

Having set ourselves on that serious aesthetic quest the problems one faces in discoursing about modern Indian art are many and varied. Traditional Indian art is characterised by two main features which distinguish it sharply from modern art. In the first place the different classical art forms of our tradition are interrelated: thus sculpture is related to dance and this in turn is related to music. Such is not the case in modern Indian art where painting is the main artistic idiom and seems unconnected to the other arts, classical or folk, performing or literary. Secondly, classical Indian art is largely mythic and therefore based on literature on the one hand and religion on the other, while this is not the case once again in modern art. Modern Indian painting is largely secular and free standing and therefore very individualistic and does not relate to any given literature, mythic or secular. When it comes to stylistic features, modern Indian art is not only figurative but can also be abstract, landscape or neo-Tantric among others. Since traditional aesthetic doctrines deal mainly with figurative art we do not have a framework of critically analysing art other than human figurative art. Landscape in Indian art is considered secondary to the human figure and Tantric forms are considered *yantras* or sacred diagrams and not high art. Evaluation of this genre of modern art is therefore difficult.

Thus it is that one must turn to the *rasa* doctrine in approaching modern Indian art. The time honoured *rasa* doctrine is not only foundational in Indian aesthetics, but since emotion is central to the human condition, a doctrine of aesthetics that bases itself on the primacy of human emotion can never be outdated. It seems prudent to approach modern Indian art through the aegis of emotion rather than through its superficial or formal features. A feature of modern art is that any set of formal criteria that we develop and that seem to apply to one artist, or school, or a movement does not apply to others. In modern art there is always a counter example to any rule or doctrine that one may establish. Hence the *rasa* doctrine, that initially accepts the formal features of art but goes beyond it to the emotion that it embodies, is the only universal doctrine that one can turn to in studying modern art.

With this in mind we approached modern Indian painting to see if in the plethora of human images that one encountered, one could discern a new primary emotion, an emotion that was not recognised by traditional Indian aesthetic doctrines, and if such a new emotion was indeed found then perhaps it could lead us into understanding some, but not all, aspects of modern art and through that emotion we might venture into an understanding of modernity itself. Makarand Paranjape, in writing about modern Indian literature, is right when he says that the old disciplinary boundaries must be questioned in our investigations. He says that "literature is no longer confined to poems, novels, short stories and plays, but also extends to embrace the critical and intellectual activity of a civilisation in several fields of scholarship including political theory, philosophy, sociology and religion."[1] While we agree with Paranjape we feel that modern Indian visual art, provides a unique window on modern civilisation even more than literature and must be considered a source for the study of Indian modernity.

In our study of modern Indian art what struck us was the fragmentation and dismemberment of the human image in the hands of some, but not all, of our modern Indian painters. It is here that we saw not only a new iconography but a new emotion and therefore a new world view. The fragmented human image was disturbingly different from the mythic *purushas* that we had learnt to adore and worship, celebrate and venerate. Not only was the human image in such paintings sharply different but the landscape and the ambience of the painting in which the image resided was anything but joyous or grand. Celestial and semi-divine beings or the sensuous and lyrical surroundings that are so much a part of traditional art were nowhere to be found. Instead one encountered banality and starkness, disorder and disarray. There was none of the tranquil smile of the Buddha, the majesty of Durgā, the loving tenderness of Pārvatī, the radiance of Naṭarāja, the magnificence of Viṣṇu, the lyrical ambience of a Pahadi miniature. Instead there were the unmistakable stigmata of despair, not just a state of psychological depression but of an utter and hopeless sense of darkness and hopelessness.

We have interpreted this state of fragmentation and darkness set in a bleak landscape as a state of existential despair, a state of godlessness, of a world where there is no cosmic justice and no hope either, of human existence that begins and ends here, of a state of mind where there is neither transcendence nor redemption.

The Indian philosophic tradition, while being joyous and optimistic about the human condition, has expressed *duḥkha* or sorrow right from the start in many different ways and in varied contexts. We have traced this *duḥkha* through the tradition and make the point that the sense of despair being expressed by modern Indian artists is both ontologically and epistemologically different from such states expressed in the past. In fact we argue that ancient *duḥkha* and modern despair are totally different and the despair as seen in the works of modern Indian artists define a certain phase of modernity for us in India.

Bharata in his Nāṭyaśāstra starts from a position of primacy of emotions and does not justify or explain them. The same is true of ancient ideas or doctrines, philosophic systems or aesthetic theories. Causality and origins, a first cause and starting points are modern, historical and Western concerns, alien to the ancient Hindu psyche, but perhaps necessary for a sociological evaluation of events and phenomena. For the ancient Hindu there was a certain beauty about acausality, a certain sanctity about events and ideas, that were not to be probed or investigated but which were to be enjoyed and realised, a certain magnificence about spontaneity or *svayaṁbhū* creations and developments. Modern historians take the position that every major idea or doctrine does not arise *de novo* but is born as a result of the socio-economic and historic conditions of the day. This type of analysis can be applied to the Indian tradition as well. Thus the rise of Buddhism in the 6th century BC, it is claimed, was distinctly related to the increase of rituals and the stratification of society on the one hand and the entrenchment of concepts and doctrines on the other.

Śaṅkara's Advaita Vedānta about a thousand years later was perhaps an outcome of the hold of Buddhism over the Indian sub-continent. Tantra, in the 10th century AD, legitimised the culture of artistic activity and pleasure seeking with a unique world view. And finally Rāmānuja's Viśiṣṭādvaita cannot be divorced from the increasing Islamic presence in the Indian civilisation at that time and the sense of alienation of the Hindus. Since we are dealing with a modern emotion in this inquiry we felt justified in investigating the unique social and economic changes in the country in the 19th and 20th centuries, which could possibly provide a backdrop to the emergence of despair in the minds of the urban artist. In taking this position we do not rule out the possibility that states of despair may arise *de novo.* The sociology of despair is dealt with by Prem Shankar Jha.

Harsha Dehejia relates the state of despair in urban intellectuals and expressed by modern artists, mainly to the onslaught of unbridled rationality that was fostered by the aggression of the white man and the British colonisation of India. However, events in post-colonial India over the last half a century have also contributed to a sense of fragmentation and alienation of the Indian mind. He feels that the art that is inspired by this sense of despair in modern India should be examined within the context of the traditional *rasa* doctrine and that a new *rasa* should be enunciated to include this *rasa* of despair in the traditional list of eight enunciated by Bharata. He further argues that recognising this *rasa* would lead us into an understanding of Indian modernity as a philosophical concept and not merely as a state of psycho-social modernisation.

Ranjit Hoskote explores a condition of mind and artistic life and writes of man's life long quest of a home. He argues that while spiritual homelessness is usually thought of as a quintessentially modern phenomenon, it has been an integral feature of the Indian cultural situation. He examines the Upaniṣads and Kālidāsā's Meghadūtam and discovers a type of homelessness in that genre of literature but it is a homeless state within a spiritual home. He notes that in the modern painter there is a contrapuntal tension between the sense of belonging and a metaphysical sense of being without location and further shows how even the modern artist having expressed the angst and anguish of a state of homelessness is prepared to define and express that state of home.

The final chapter explores possible post-modern reactions to this state of modern despair and once again looks at modern Indian painting to find this. While the paradigm of post-modern discourse is a collage or montage, certain post-modern images in India express a certain playfulness and bring together, without a clearly defined border, the profound and the banal, and in so doing create a non-space, a state of animation without a defining emotion.

ENDNOTE

1. Makarand Paranjape: Towards a New Literary History: Indian English Literature. Horizons, Volume XXXXXVI, Numbers 1 and 2. Indian Council for Cultural Relations. New Delhi.

2

THE SOCIOLOGY OF DESPAIR

Prem Shankar Jha

Despair is sorrow unredeemed by hope. It is a powerful emotion born of irreparable loss, that modern man is familiar with. It is therefore all the more surprising that it finds no place in the ten *rasas* that are the building blocks of the Indian system of aesthetics. Why is this so? One reason, almost certainly, is that despair is an individual emotion. The emotions depicted by the ten *rasas* are universal ones. The purpose of the *rasa* theory is to create a base of shared emotions that unites not only the artist with his audience, not only the members of the audience with each other, but also the different art forms themselves, in a single unified, creative whole. Such a grand attempt at synthesis is only possible in a society that also has a holistic vision of itself; in which not just all humans, but the entire natural world is perceived as a single indivisible whole, to be cherished and protected. That is, of course, the essence of *dharma*, the bedrock of Hinduism.

In such a society, men and women are connected to each other through the intangible but ever present web of social relations. Emotions are shared. Those that are so powerfully individualistic as to be considered disruptive are discouraged through custom and taboo, and their manifestation often punished. In such societies individualism is discounted, usually discouraged. The good of the community takes precedence over the desires of the individual. The other face of this wholeness is that grief and loss, the death of a loved one, an economic setback, a natural calamity, too are shared. The ultimate sustenance is that of religion, the church and its liturgy, the Brahmin's discourse on the banks of a river, the *guru* and the *ṛṣi*. It is religion, philosophy and the bonds of community that between them lift the burden of sorrow, and create space for resignation, ultimately acceptance. Each powerful experience of this kind only reinforces the bonds of the individual with the society to which he belongs. In such societies despair may be born, but it is not allowed to live.

The harmony, the universality of shared experience, which is reflected in the *rasa* theory is not confined to India. Although Western civilization had no counterpart to it, from the middle ages to the end of the eighteenth century, its music and art reflect the same urge towards universality. Not surprisingly, religious themes dominate Western art. The artist is subordinated to his art. The identity of Russian and Flemish icon painters, for example, is often not known, any more than that of the sculptors of Chartres, even though their art limns the walls and reredos' of the grandest European churches. A typical concert of Elizabethan music is likely to contain more than one piece by composers whose names are not known. Expressions of individualism in art were limited by a strictness of form. Adherence to form guaranteed universality of appreciation. In European art and music of the pre-modern period too, one finds piety, devotion, fear, awe, anger, tenderness, love, but not despair. Only towards the end of this period did individuality begin to creep in. There is passion in the music of Johan Sebastian Bach, as there is a profound all-encompassing serenity in that of Handel, but one has to be a discerning listener to perceive it.

When, and where did despair make its entry? As was mentioned above, despair is an individual, a highly personal emotion. The social change that gives birth to it, is the rise of individualism and the slow dissolution of the bonds of society. And the rise of individualism is indissolubly linked to the rise of commercial and then industrial Capitalism.

The link may not be obvious. Is Capitalism not just another form of economic organization of society, one that supplanted feudalism and mercantilism? What does it have to do with art? The answer is that Capitalism devastated society, tearing loose the bonds that united men with men and left them to fend for themselves in a frightening new world. All this was justified in the name of freedom. Liberty and equality became the clarion calls of the rising bourgeoisie of Europe as it sought to break the chains of the mercantilist state. The individual was born in this cauldron of change. But even that was only the effect of a still more fundamental change that Capitalism wrought. This was to drastically reverse the organizing principle of society itself.

Prior to the Capitalist epoch, from early pre-history, human society shunned competition, which was perceived as being disruptive of social relations. The institution within which man competed with man was the market. As a result markets, although ubiquitous in early societies, were carefully circumscribed by ritual and taboo. Relations within a social group were based not on competition but on the principles of reciprocity and redistribution. This was especially true of economic relations. Reciprocity, and not barter was the primary mode of exchange of goods and services. The origins of reciprocity lay in the division of functions within the family, but blossomed in an extraordinary variety of ways as social organizations became more complex. In some societies reciprocity meant that men provided food and other articles to their sisters and their children, while their wives were similarly taken care of by their matrilineal relatives. This was as true of supposedly primitive Trobriand Islanders of Western Melanesia as of the highly advanced Nairs of Kerala. In others, entire villages developed reciprocal or dual relations with others, exchanging for instance, fish for fruit. Such rings of exchange attained an enormous complexity in several island societies. This was trade on a grand scale but based not on competition but reciprocity.[1]

Redistribution meant sharing the product of one's economic activity with the community to which one belonged. The commonest manifestations were the sharing of the spoils of war, the yields of the hunt, the catch of fish, the pick of fruit, the harvesting of crops, and so on. Redistribution grew out naturally from the fact that hunting, fishing and going into the jungle to gather fruit were communally shared activities. Thus it was difficult to define how much each person's individual contribution had been. In early societies the commonest form of redistribution was the surrender of a part of the product to the headman or chief who would distribute it among all the members of the tribe. Like reciprocity, redistribution also took a wide variety of forms as social organizations grew more complex.

Both reciprocity and redistribution therefore required a specific form of social organization to support it. In the case of the latter, it required a considerable delegation of authority to a tribal elder or chief, whose decisions on how the produce would be distributed were above dispute. Add to the above two principles, the fact that the dominant mode of production was production for use, within the family or household, where the authority of the father, and sometimes the mother, was rarely questioned, and it becomes apparent that social organization in the pre-Capitalist epoch tended naturally towards a strong centralization of authority. The most evolved form of this type of society was the monarchy.

Capitalism replaced reciprocity and redistribution with competition as the organizing principle of society. It did this because the driving motive of Capitalism was personal gain or profit. Competition first appeared in foreign trade, which was the least amenable to control by law, custom or taboo. Indeed, trade itself grew out of the most vicious competition of all, war, and in its earliest manifestation was often indistinguishable from plunder. As commerce developed between the growing urban centers within countries, it also appeared in domestic trade. Manufacture was controlled during the medieval period by guilds, which had their own elaborate systems for the prevention of competition. It was only the growth of international trade that permitted individual merchants to set up manufacturing facilities outside the guilds. This was the origin of the 'putting out' system.

The first markets in which competition prevailed were international ones. Domestic trade even between cities, remained carefully circumscribed , and elaborate arrangements were made to keep it separate from international trade. It was only through the conscious intervention of the emerging nation State that the barriers between the two were broken down, and a national market gradually developed, which began to integrate the countryside with the towns through the medium of trade.

The rise of trade and manufacture led to the growth of towns, and in them to the emergence of the bourgeoisie. It was the bourgeoisie that hailed the loosening of social bonds that resulted from urbanization, as the dawn of freedom for the individual. However, it was not till the advent of the machine that Capitalism fully transformed the organizing principle of society. During the phase of commercial Capitalism, markets had grown and the barriers between domestic and international markets had gradually been eroded, but these were still markets for commodities. Land and labor, which came later to be called factors of production remained outside the system of exchange.

The machine, with its enormous productivity, made hitherto undreamed of demands on the Capitalist to develop markets where his products could be absorbed, and to ensure a steady supply of raw materials to feed, and workers to tend, to the machines. What is more, since demand waxed and waned because of what economists later came to recognize as trade cycles, both the workers and the raw materials had to be 'on tap', free to be hired and fired at will. The needs of the machine, therefore, led to the commercialization of land and the conversion of human beings into labor. From being outside the system of exchange, land and human beings became a part of it, commodities that could be bought and sold like any other.

This development was and remains unique to the present age. In all previous ages, markets had been no more than accessories to economic life which was organized around principles like reciprocity, redistribution and the household as the center of production. When national markets did develop and attained a high level of sophistication as during the period of mercantilism, they were strongly regulated. The service of the machine required that all these regulations be scrapped, and one single law govern the entire market, that of supply and demand. This was not a law devised by a human agency, be it guild, Burgess or Crown, but one devised by the market itself. Polanyi has called this the self-regulating market.[2]

The progress of industrial Capitalism spelt the triumph of the self-regulating market over all previous forms of economic organization. Since most of those had been devised to curb competition, the triumph of the machine and the rise of the self-regulating market meant the victory of competition. Thus parallel to the triumph of the law of supply and demand, Capitalism ensured the rise to dominance of one motive, that of gain or profit. Competition, the route to profit, thus became the single most important organizing principle of the economy. In England, the change was quite sudden, and took place around 1780, between Adam Smith's writing of *The Wealth of Nations, and Townsend's Dissertation on the Poor Laws.* "The former marked the close of an age which opened with the inventors of the State, Thomas More and Machiavelli, Luther and Calvin: the latter belonged to that 19th century in which Ricardo and Hegel discovered from opposite angles the existence of a society that was not subject to the laws of the State, but, on the contrary, subjected the State to its own laws."[3]

The self-regulating market devastated society. It did this by firmly subordinating the needs of human beings to those of the machine. To be freely available, labor had to be mobile. But to be mobile it had to be torn free of the shackles of family, village, parish, and even country and continent. Relentlessly therefore Capitalism stripped human beings of their social identities and their social protection, and reduced them to their irreducible biological selves. It was this fragmented self that was given the exalted title of the 'individual'.

The effect that the rise of the self-regulating market had on society has been described in exhaustive detail and need not detain us long. The commercialization of agriculture and the repeal of laws that had bound workers to their home villages and Parishes in England, provided a ready supply of labor to the mills, but the rise and fall of demand meant that some portion of these workers were out of work for much of the time. This gave rise to the phenomenon of pauperism, a phenomenon that had visited England during the first enclosure movement in the 15th and 16th centuries, but was otherwise unknown till the advent of the machine.

The fact that so many of those who gravitated to towns in

search of work left their families behind in the villages, and that those who found themselves out of work had to resort to desperate stratagems to keep themselves alive, turned the cities into cesspools of vice and crime. Everywhere, hitherto undreamed of wealth, itself the product of the machine, co-existed with undreamed of misery and degradation. However, what Capitalism was doing to society in its home countries paled into insignificance before the ravages it visited on those it colonized. In the latter it decimated entire races and civilizations through forced labor, malnutrition and disease, destroyed the livelihoods of millions of artisans, destroyed indigenous patterns of agriculture, and tore apart the jungle to create plantations that would feed the 'Satanic mills'. It also tore loose millions upon millions of human beings from the bosom of their families and communities in Africa, China, and India, to send them as slaves and indentured labor to work the new mines and plantations in far off lands. To the poor of that epoch it must have seemed that God, in whom they had placed their trust, and on whom they depended for succor in times of grief and need, had turned his face away from them.

Despair was thus born with the birth of 'the individual'. But its consolidation into a *rasa* that appeared more and more frequently in the arts and indeed permeated entire epochs of creative endeavor, can be traced to the realization that God had failed mankind. A new force was loose in society, whose iron laws were as implacable as those of God, but it was one that, unlike God knew no mercy. People could pray to, bargain with or hope for propitiation from God but not from this new force. This was the market. Today, the notion of the individual is so much a part of the very warp of our thinking, and individualism is so unquestioningly deemed a virtue, that it is very difficult to visualize a time when this was not so. Yet at the end of the 17th century, the notion of the individual human being, the biologically defined human entity that the new liberal creed of the era pitted against society or the State, was still relatively new and indeed revolutionary. The breaking of the constraints of society released individual energies in a manner that the world had never known. But for every winner, there were a thousand losers. And the implacability of the market deprived the losers of hope.

Despair began to surface in the arts and literature of Europe in the second half of the nineteenth century. The change is visible in the contrast between the early and late music of Mozart, whose differences go far beyond those that can be attributed to age and self-confidence. Mozart's early music hews closely to the Rococo tradition. Much of it is music to suit specific occasions, written for specific patrons, and intended to please. His individualism and budding genius has to be actively looked for in the finer points of composition and inventiveness. The late music, by contrast, is far more expressive of Mozart's feelings, makes greater and more effective use of somber keys like C Minor, D Minor and G Minor, and more than once, as in the second movement of the 23rd Piano concerto, plunges into something close to despair. His last, unfinished work, the Requiem, is also the darkest, and is written so much for himself that the requirements or indeed the identity of the patron, becomes unimportant.

A decade after his death, Beethoven celebrated the rise of Napoleon, whom he considered the exemplar of the heroic individual who breaks the shackles of state and society, in his Eroica symphony. Not entirely coincidentally, the second movement of that symphony, a funeral march, comes as close to an expression of despair as anything Beethoven ever wrote. Much of Beethoven's music, especially his larger works, is preoccupied with the struggle of the individual against an overwhelming and malign fate. Despair peeps out repeatedly from the late music of Schubert, who outlived Beethoven by only a few years but belonged to the next generation of composers. It is ever present in his lieder, in the late string quartets and his final string quintet. Again not coincidentally, Romanticism in European music sought to liberate music from the shackles of form in order to liberate the human individual soul.

Despair attained its full artistic flowering in the late 19th century. It is ever present in the paintings of the Russian social realists like Pegov, and in the late music of Tschaikovsky, notably the Symphonie Pathetique. But the inseparability of individualism, of freedom, and despair, is most sharply highlighted in literature. Nowhere is this more so than in the novels of Dostoyevsky. In *Crime and Punishment*, in *The Brothers Karamazov*, and in *The Possessed*, he obsessively explores the moral limits of individual freedom, and all these novels are limned by an undercurrent of despair. It was left finally to the 20th century, to a Chagall or an Antonin Artaud, to treat despair as the main, even the sole, subject matter of art.

Indian art and music have not traveled the entire route that European art has travelled, because Capitalism is still in its relatively early stages. Individualism in music and dance have emerged with the growth of audiences and the transfer of the art forms from the court and temple to the public stage. The subscription concerts of Vienna in the early 19th century are finding their echo in the ticketed performances in public auditoria to which the new Indian bourgeoisie of the cities are flocking. Not surprisingly such public performances are most frequent in Bombay and Calcutta, the most industrialized and commercialized of Indian cities, while patronage continues to hold sway in Delhi and smaller towns. With the emergence of the public performance, individualism has crept into music and dance. Experimentation with form and content is increasing and even artistes who hew to traditional forms express occasional impatience with its strictures. But the dominance of tradition in music and dance has so far prevented the expression of despair in that art form. Not surprisingly it is in painting, the most individual of art forms, and in literature, that individualism and despair have surfaced.

The purpose of this paper is not to discuss the emergence of despair in Indian art and literature, but to trace the impact of Capitalism on Indian society, which set the stage for its emergence. Prior to the advent of the British, India had a traditional but rich economic life. Agriculture was the main occupation, but at least a fifth, perhaps a quarter of the population was engaged in artisanal industry, wherein textiles dominated. The land tenure system was perfected by the Mughals. All the land belonged in principle to the Emperor, and was leased or farmed out to intermediaries. The farmer was a subtenant many times removed from the owner of the land, but the terms of his tenure were ultimately regulated by royal fiat, and were on the whole benign. Rent was collected, for instance, on the land actually cultivated and not leased, and took account of the nature of the harvest. Control over rapacious intermediaries was exercised by the threat of changing them, for the right to collect land revenue could be revoked and given to someone else.

Artisanal industry was not a subsistence activity, for it did not meet the needs of the household, or the immediate local market, be it village or market town. A good part of its products was bought by the nobility of the large towns and cities, and was of extraordinary quality. A national market, or at least several regional markets, therefore existed, and was serviced by a vast, elaborate network of moneylenders. The British transferred funds from Bengal to western India to finance the Maratha wars through Benares based moneylenders.

There can be little doubt that the impact of trade with European nations during the pre-colonial epoch was a beneficial one. The British bought mainly fine cotton textiles, and paid for it with silver bullion. The inflow of silver had an expansionary effect on the three regional economies, from which all benefitted. The weavers in particular prospered. By the end of the 18th century as many as 40,000 looms worked for the company. This may have been as many as a tenth of the total number of looms working in the Madras Presidency.[4] Weavers prospered in Bengal too. For in addition to the Mughal nobility, they had a steady buyer of their high value-added products in the East India Company.

How drastically the situation changed when the British began to rule India, may be judged from what happened in Bengal after the British victory in the Battle of Plassey in 1757. The indiscriminate plunder that followed immediately robbed the handicraft industry, especially the weavers, of one of their main sources of patronage. But something worse happened: administrative control gave the British the right to levy tribute from the land that had previously gone to the Mughal State. This freed the East India Company of the need to bring in silver. Henceforth, it had enough resources to not only meet the costs of administration and finance its future conquests, but also to finance its exports. From 1765, therefore, silver ceased to be imported into Bengal. An imperfect idea of the resulting deflation may be had from the fact that while cowries, the poor man's currency in Mughal India, had held their value in relation to silver for three centuries, depreciated by almost half between 1803 and 1835.[5] By that time silver had not only stopped being imported but was also being exported, along with opium, to finance the Company's trade with China.

To make matters worse, the British introduced a number of improvements to the administration of land reforms that increased the yield of the land revenue without any corresponding increase in agricultural produce. Thus, whereas the Mughal administration had levied tribute on the land actually cultivated in a given year, the British levied it on the land leased by a farmer irrespective of whether he was able to get a crop from it or not. Mughal administration was also flexible in its collection of land revenue, for it tended to excuse or lower payment when there was a drought or flood. The East India Company was not so forgiving. As a result, land revenue turned, by degrees, into a fixed cost of agriculture, a first charge that was transferred by the Zamindars on to the shoulders of the cultivator, who had to bear all the risks of cultivation. Over successive cycles of drought and flood this could not have failed to impoverish the peasantry. The scales were loaded more firmly against the cultivator when the East India company, which now needed silver to finance its China trade as once it had needed it to finance its trade with India, decided to demonetize the cowrie and accept only silver, and that too in the form of a particular *sicca.*

This led to a large loss of accumulated savings for the poor whose only form of capital was the *cowrie.* But since this was done when the value of silver was rising sharply, all the costs of conversion into a relatively high denomination, and, therefore, increasingly cumbersome, medium of exchange, were borne once more, by the cultivator.[6] The overall effect of the British victory at Plassey was not only the physical expropriation of the accumulated past savings of the nobility, and the destruction, at least in part of the savings of ordinary people, but also a relentless erosion of agriculture's capacity to generate savings in the future.

In 1813, the British Parliament passed a Charter act that ended the East India Company's monopoly of trade with India. From then onwards, Lancashire cotton textiles began to be imported into India. According to one view this did not harm the Indian weaver anywhere near as much as the classical economic historians believed, because the main benefit of mechanization was to lower the cost of producing yarn. Cheaper yarn enabled Indian weavers to bring down their cloth prices. This and the increase in population helped to cushion the impact of the import of machine made textiles.[7] The precise extent to which it did so has not been estimated, but there can be no doubt that weavers would have had to lower prices substantially, even when using imported yarn, to compete with mill-made cloth.[8] For most weavers, the competition proved too severe. By 1837, a bare 20 years after imports were allowed, Lancashire cotton had taken over about six per cent of the domestic market for textiles[9]. This continued throughout the century and continues to the present day, although the culprit from the closing years of the 19th century was the indigenous modern textiles industry. What was happening in the textiles industry was being mirrored in other industries. The industrial segment of the population of Gangetic Bihar fell from 18.6 per cent in 1809 to 8.5 per cent in 1901.[10]

Even the above figures have been disputed on methodological grounds, but one does not need extensive data from the past to surmise the long, slow death of the handloom based textiles industry. Even when weavers were not forced out of work they were marginalised and impoverished. What happened to them in the 19th century is similar to what is happening to the older power loom industry in the Indian decentralized sector today, after the lifting of curbs on the expansion of the composite mills and the emergence of a decentralized but extremely modern weaving sector in Indian textiles. They were forced to cater increasingly to the poorer segments of the population. They had to make do on smaller and smaller profit margins, and became vulnerable to even small shifts in input prices or declines in the purchasing power of their customers. It is ironic that the very same people who devised international trade protocols to protect their dying textiles industries in the post-war period gave no such protection to the textiles industry in India a century and a half earlier. It is not necessary to add that no matter what its power might once have been, such a dying industry could scarcely generate surpluses that could be channeled into modern industrialization. When modern industry did finally begin to take root in India, it came into headlong conflict with the British policy of free trade. This was never a product of altruism. Contrary to what a later generation of economists had to say, the British policy makers of the mid-19th century were never in doubt that free trade by their country was meant to retard industrialization by its rivals.

In the 1840s, the British Board of Trade justified its support for the repeal of the corn laws on the grounds that the opportunity to sell wheat freely to Britain would divert German capital, which was being driven into industry back into agriculture, and thus retard German industrialization. But since Germany and France were independent countries, the British could only offer inducements to them not to industrialize. In the case of India, it could prevent industrialization by specific edict. Thus as Europe and the United States raised tariff walls against British goods, Britain sought to compensate by tightening its hold on the markets of its colonies. The British did not stop there but altered other policies to nip any threat of industrialization in the bud. Thus, in 1882, all Tarriffs on imports from the United Kingdom were abolished. This did not overwhelm the infant Indian textile industry because the import of silver and its minting into coins in India was free. This led to a steady devaluation of the rupee which continued to give the Indian industry protection against imports. However that phase lasted only till 1893, when the British banned the minting of coins, except at government mints. The slower growth of money supply set off a deflation and led to the revaluation of the rupee from 13.1d. (old pence) in 1894-5, to 16d. in 1898-9 (Rupees fifteen to the Pound).[11] The denial of protection and other methods of discouraging Indian industrialization continued till 1946, a year before Independence. In 1907, when the Tata Iron and Steel Company was founded, the British remained deaf to pleas for protection. As a result, it was 16 years before the company was able to declare its first dividend. Despite the interruption of supplies during two World Wars, the Indian railways never took advantage of the sizable engineering industry that had grown up in India to meet any of its main needs. They were throughout encouraged to buy British to the point where they did not use their own workshops to build locomotives.[12] During the second World War, the interruption of supplies from the United Kingdom and the advance of the Japanese to the gates of Assam, created the conditions for the rise of a machine tools industry in India mainly to meet the war needs for small arms and ammunition of the allied army. Four machine tools companies grew and thrived on this demand during the war. But no sooner was it over than the British once more denied protection to the machine tools makers. New machines flooded in from the United Kingdom. By 1947, three of the four companies had gone out of business. The fourth, Kirloskars, survived by switching to the manufacture of oil engines.[13]

Perhaps most insidious of all was the change in the structure of the Indian economy wrought by two centuries of colonialism. From being an exporter of manufactured cloth, India turned in the 19th century, into an exporter of raw cotton. Even as agriculture designed to meet the needs of the local population, languished, an export oriented, plantation sector emerged, to supply cotton, jute, indigo, tea and coffee to the world market. Plantation agriculture did not, admittedly, wreak the havoc in India that it wreaked in parts of Central and South America, but some of it, as in the case of jute and indigo, replaced food crops for domestic market and further increased pressure on the land. And while plantation agriculture was profitable, once more the surpluses stayed almost entirely in European hands. The emergence of cash crop and plantation agriculture was only one aspect of its commercialization. The other was the commercialization of food crops, made possible by the railways.

The railways made it possible to move foodgrain very long distances and therefore, directly benefitted the growth of large urban centers like Calcutta and Bombay. But the enlarged market increased the power of money to suck surpluses out of the countryside. In times of scarcity, prices rose in the rural areas by far more than in the towns, a phenomenon we see till this day, and the rural poor starved. It is not surprising that India was racked by a series of famines in the last quarter of the 19th century, i.e. after much of the railway network had been laid down. The worst of these, in 1896-97, affected 96 million people and caused an estimated 5.1 million deaths. Thus, the Bengal famine of 1943, which was caused not so much by an absolute shortage of food, but by the unrestricted access to rural surpluses given to Calcutta based traders by a British government intent on supplying food to the British army at any cost, was not unique, but only the last of a long series of disasters caused by the commercialization of agriculture. The cycle of famines rapidly widened income differentials in the rural areas and changed the structure of land ownership and tenancy for the worse. Every famine led to the impoverishment of the already weak, who had few if any hoards of foodgrain and were forced to sell first their cattle and then their land to survive. Thus, every famine concentrated the ownership of land, and added to the numbers of landless laborers. Studies of South India by Dharma Kumar show that the proportion of agricultural laborers increased from about 15 to 17 per cent at the beginning of the 19th century to 27 to 29 per cent at its end.

Here, too, one needs to distinguish between the impact of commercialization and that of colonial rule. Commercialization is beneficial if it accompanies increases in agricultural productivity. That was what happened in Japan and is happening in much of India today under the spur of the green revolution. But it is destructive if it is superimposed on a stagnant agriculture as happened in 19th century India. Colonialism played no small part in ensuring that agriculture did indeed remain stagnant.

The decay of the villages, which accompanied the destruction of artisanal industry, and the commercialization of a by and large stagnant agriculture, was accompanied by a parallel decay of the towns. Throughout the 19th century, Calcutta, Bombay and Madras recorded steady growths of population, but virtually every other town, from Dhaka to Moradabad, Lucknow and Murshidabad shrank, in some cases to less than half its original size.[14] These were the centers for, and in which the artisans had produced their finest wares. The impoverishment, and then disappearance of the nobility, and the onslaught of British mill made products sealed their doom. There could be no better evidence of the disintegration of the economic and social life of pre-Capitalist India.

The evidence is, therefore, compelling. India entered the Capitalist age as a victim of the market and not as its beneficiary. As nations went, it was one of Capitalism's losers, not winners. Not surprisingly, despair also entered Indian art as a *leitmotif* in the 19th century. It did so in the new art of the large, emerging metropolis, and in forms of literature such as drama, the novel and the short story, that also reflected the rise of individualism in Indian creative arts. However, the counterpart of despair in European art, the exaltation of the individual and the celebration of his victory over the forces of destiny, is almost wholly absent. That is perhaps the difference between being a victor and a victim.

ENDNOTES

1. Karl Polanyi: The Great Transformation: Beacon Press, Boston, Mass. 1957. Chapter 4, p. 50 The Kula Ring in Western Melanesia, based on the principle of reciprocity, is one of the most elaborate trading transactions known to man.
2. ibid. Chapter 6.
3. ibid.
4. This ratio, calculated by Dodwell and accepted by Habib (*op cit*) is questioned by Dharma Kumar. However it does not seem unreasonable.
5. Bagchi, *op cit* p. 504, quoting K.P. Mitra: Currency of Orissa, published in Bengal Past and Present, July-December 1939.

6. Bagchi: *op cit.*
7. M.D. Morris: Cambridge Economic History of India, Volume 2, p. 669.
8. Meghnad Desai: in The Indian Economic and Social History Review, Volume VIII (4) p. 354. Quoted by Habib *op cit.* Desai estimated that weavers would have had to raise productivity or accept a decline in prices of 43% to compete with mill made cloth. This would imply an even sharper decline in net earning.
9. Habib, *op cit.* p. 361.
10. Bagchi: Deindustrialisation in India in the Nineteenth Century: some theoretical implications. Journal of Development Studies, 1976, Volume 12. Number 2.
11. Habib, *op cit.* p. 379.
12. Amiya Kumar Bagchi: The Political Economy of Underdevelopment. Cambridge University Press 1982.
13. Private communication by Dr. S.M. Patil, Chairman of Hindustan Machine Tools (since renamed HMT) in September 1976.
14. Habib, *op cit.*

3

FROM ANCIENT DUHKHA TO MODERN DESPAIR

Harsha V. Dehejia

Discourse on *duḥkha**, ordinarily translated as suffering, forms an important part of all three Indian philosophical systems namely Hindu, Buddhist and Jain. Equally, it was a part of the oral tradition transmitted by our itinerant performers and story tellers. So integral is the concept of *duḥkha* in the Indian tradition that it is situated within the ambit of the discourse on the human condition and predicament and takes the form of intense questioning of what it is to be a human. *Mokṣa*, understood as perfect or self-knowledge requires not only a recognition but equally an acceptance of *duḥkha*. While different traditions vary in the emphasis attached to *duḥkha*, none of the traditions by-pass it in their quest of ultimate self-realisation. Thus while the Buddha emphatically declared *sarvaṁ duḥkham*, the Upaniṣads put it softly when they state that suffering is *avidyā*, ignorance.

At the outset, it is important to state that the Indian philosophic tradition is elitist in its approach and in its expectation of those who venture into it. The entire edifice of Indian philosophy is built upon some fundamental foundations or presuppositions. The *karma* doctrine, understood in its many different nuances, is a tacit presupposition of all Indian systems of philosophy. Equally importantly, ancient Indian philosophers, from the *ṛṣis* of the Vedas downwards address themselves to higher rather than to mundane concerns, to one who has mastered the material and

* I am indebted to Prof. Prabodh Parikh for the many discussions I have had with him on this subject.

emotional needs of life and who is now engaged in spiritual pursuits, to one who is craving for the intoxication of higher knowledge and not one who is still caught up in the struggle of existence, to the *rājā* rather than the *prajā*. Karl Potter is right when he says that Indian philosophy is essentialist rather than existentialist and should be called *mokṣaśāstra* or the science of liberation meant for one who has fully realised, mastered and celebrated life.

It is thus that ontic or *saṁsāric duḥkha*, though important to the human body and mind, does not engage the attention of Indian philosophers to any significant extent except perhaps in the Sāṁkhya system. The body is subject to disease, death and decay and the mind to delusion, anxiety and fear. All of these conditions undoubtedly lead to malaise and melancholy but neither of these are fit subjects for a serious philosophic inquiry. They are best left to doctors and psychiatrists. In ancient India, the understanding and treatment of these ailments was left to shamans and faith healers, elders and medicine men. The history of these ailments, the way they were perceived and handled, treated and resolved in the Indian tradition would make an interesting study but cannot occupy our attention here. This study would involve looking into a variety of folk beliefs and practices, bring us face to face with godmen and medicine men, the *rājā* and the *prajā*, royalty and proleteriat, for bodily and mental afflictions spared no one. Important and interesting as these problems are, they should not distract our attention and lead us away from the central concern of philosophy. It has been rightly said *sarvaśāstra-prayojanam ātmadarśanam*, the purpose of philosophy is to obtain a vision of our transcendent self. Using the *Naṭarāja* as our visual paradigm of knowledge, transcendence involves lifting ourselves away, like the uplifted left foot of the *Naṭarāja*, from the cycle of *sṛṣṭi*, *sthiti* and *saṁhāra* or creation, maintenance and destruction of life and rising above the snare of earthly *māyā* as portrayed by the right foot. Our task, if we are to understand *duḥkha*, is to come to terms with the *apasmāra* upon which the *Naṭarāja* dances.

Duḥkha, in its true and philosophic sense and in keeping with the elitist nature of all philosophic inquiry and especially Indian, should not be understood as suffering or pain, neither as misery nor misfortune nor as torment or travail. These English words give a pale, negative, pessimistic and limited view of the concept of *duḥkha*. *Duḥkha* in the Indian philosophic tradition is an exalted state of being that arises from a sense of limitation in the upward and onward reach of the radiant consciousness, it is a state of joyous expectation while waiting for the final step of enlightenment, it is the eagerness of a devotee longing for a vision of the divine, the anxiety of the *nāyikā* who has realised her love but who is anxious for the final embrace with her *nāyaka*, the tension of the poet who has written a beautiful song and needs to write the concluding line, for the person who has led a rich and celebratory life and is looking for the final realisation of *mokṣa*. Understood in this light, ontic pain of the human condition hardly merits any discussion. *Duḥkha*, therefore, must arise from *sukha*, it is complimentary not antagonistic to *sukha*, and in this sense *sukha* and *duḥkha* are *mithuna*, two states of the human mind that must be looked upon like a loving couple in a blissful embrace, and must not be understood as suffering in its very limited and banal sense. *Duḥkha* ennobles and chastens man in his effort at spiritual regeneration or *pūrṇatva*, wholeness. On this concept of suffering, it would be useful to quote Radhakrishnan at length:

> When man struggles to free himself from his natural entanglements, life becomes intense with strife. Suffering is the condition of progress. Struggle is the law of existence and sacrifice the principle of evolution. The more the struggle and sacrifice, the greater are the joy and the freedom ... Suffering is the ransom the son of man has to pay if he would attain his crown. It reveals to us the incomplete nature of the self and the world ... Suffering is the messenger of God revealing to us the importance of the world, the episodic nature of earthly life. (Suffering) drives the soul to put forth its whole strength and thus compels it to grow. The darker the sky the brighter will the stars shine. Suffering cannot be abolished so long as

> spiritual life has to be lived under human conditions. Until the whole being is made an offering to God the process of gradual rise through suffering cannot cease ... Life is a place of torment where the human spirit writhes to possess the eternal. Veil after veil is to be withdrawn. The illusions of life are to be torn away and our cherished dreams dispersed before the divine life can be reached.[1]

Duḥkha, therefore, is not something to be abolished or shunned but to be courted and embraced in the human quest for perfection.

The Vedas do not engage in any systematic philosophic discourse although a number of fundamental ideas in seminal form are to be found in the hymns. Within its joyous and life affirming ambience, one finds cryptic hints of what is later developed into a major thesis. Of special interest in our search for the concept of *duḥkha,* is the firm assertion by the Vedic *ṛṣi,* that *puruṣa* reveals only a quarter of himself while three fourths lie hidden, suggesting the inability of rational intellectual activity to grasp *puruṣa,* an idea of great epistemic importance which is taken up later in the Upaniṣads. However, while the Vedic poets radiantly engage themselves in eulogising the beauty of life around them, such as that of the life giving sun and its chariot, the primordial waters and the cow that fulfils their needs, it is in the *Nāsadīya sūkta* that the *ṛṣi* raises the primal question of creation: *tso aṅga veda yadi vā na veda,* he truly knows it or he does not even know, a question that is not a renunciation of knowledge or of existential despair but an admission that the question is beyond the scope of rational knowledge, a courageous admission that not everything can be known by the human mind, and that despite this the ardent inquiry into ultimate reality and the quest for perfect knowledge and its realisation must go on. For, notwithstanding the inability to reach this knowledge the *ṛṣis* chant the cry of victory: "we have drunk the Soma and become immortal. We have attained the light, We have found the Gods." It is the final refrain of the *puruṣa sūkta* that establishes the Vedic poets as radiant knowledge seekers: *vedāham etam puruṣam mahāntam ādityavarnaṁ tamasaḥ parastāt,* I have known this mighty *puruṣa* who is refulgent as the sun beyond darkness, *tameva viditvāti-mṛtyumeti nānyaḥ panthāḥ vidyate'yanāya,* by knowing him alone one transcends death, there is no other way to go. If there is *duḥkha* in the Vedas it is in the ardent wish not to be denied *cakṣurno dehi,* divine vision.

The Upaniṣads embark on a systematic journey of discovery, not through a revelation but contemplation, not by seeking supernatural powers but through a courageous and radiant search for ultimate reality, a heroic effort to move from the apparent to the real, form darkness to light and from death to immortality. The early Upaniṣads pick up where the Vedas leave off and set their discourse within the ambit of *brahman* and *ātman.* The fundamental problem, and, therefore, a central source of *duḥkha* in the Upaniṣads, is that while there is *brahman-ātman* homology, or in other words that while *brahman* and *ātman* are ontologically the same, there is for the embodied being a gulf, not only between the *ātman* and the *brahman,* but between what is attainable by the senses and the intellect and the greater reality that lies beyond it. The *brahman* seeking student is told in no uncertain terms that the ultimate and radiant *brahman* that the student is seeking, is nothing but his very own *ātman,* a strident declaration that leads to the *mahāvākya,* a quintessential Upaniṣadic dictum *tat tvam asi,* That Thou Art.

This is the glorious discovery of the *ṛṣis* and this equally becomes the source of *duḥkha,* for the destination is known but the path to it is unclear, the will to uncover that truth is present but it is the very light of that blazing reality that seems to blind the seeker. The drive towards *advaita* from a position of *dvaita,* of the quest of the spirit although entrenched in matter, of the wish to see the sun in all its refulgence although living in flickerings of light, of the ardent desire to move from the *savikalpa brahman* revealed by the senses and the intellect to the glorious *nirvikalpa brahman* above and beyond sensual perceptions and intellectual activity, is the central mission of the Upaniṣads and the stress to fulfill this by the *brahmajijñāsu,* the seeker of knowledge, the only source of his *duḥkha.* These two *brahmans,* the numinal and the phenomenal, the *nirvikalpa* and *savikalpa*, the yon and the actual, we are told in the Śvetāśvatara Upaniṣad, are both real and are like two birds of the self same feathers, one eating sweet fruit which is deluded while the other watches and remains serene. The tension between the two *brahmans*, according to the Upaniṣads, is to be resolved by a process of systematic negation, *neti neti*, negating the lower for the higher, the conceptual for what lies beyond thought constructs, the immediate for the ultimate. The diversity and the manifoldness of this world as revealed by the six senses is to be resolved into the oneness of *advaya*, that which is without a second. The problem for the seeker and, therefore, a source of his *duḥkha* is, having known the eye, to go to the eye of the eye and having known the mind to go to the *manaso manaḥ*, the mind of the mind. For, it is easy to rest in the mind but to do so would be to seek the reflection of the sun in turbid and restless waters or be satisfied with flickerings of that radiant light. There is no resting for the ardent seeker till he reaches the stillness and vastness, the beauty and the grandeur, the radiance and the refulgence of the yonder mind, the mind of the mind, and hence the petition by the *ṛṣi* to remove the golden lid that covers the face of the truth, *hiraṇmayena pātreṇa satyasya pihitam mukham.* And to be put onto that path of spiritual riches the seeker petitions Agni, the fire of consciousness, *agne naya supathā rāye.* This is hardly a prayer to be released from the ontic pain of the human condition. It is in this ardent prayer and petition that the *duḥkha* of the Upaniṣads is to be understood.

Śaṅkara in his *Vivekacūḍāmaṇī*[2] calls the strength and resolve of the seeker to endure this *duḥkha* without anxiety or lament as *titikṣā.* For Śaṅkara the problem, and, therefore, the source of *duḥkha* for the Vedāntin, is the limitation of his *savikalpa jñāna*, knowledge that is gained from sense perception and ratiocination, to capture the essence of *nirvikalpa brahman.* Not only is the *savikalpa jñāna* limited but binds the seeker to the phenomenal world and subjects him to the heat and delusion of *saṁsāra* and, therefore, leads to dissatisfaction and disenchantment. For *buddhi* has *doṣas* (#355) or limitations and it is *buddhi* which prevents the realisation of *nitya* eternal, *advaya* non-dual, *akhaṇḍa* unbroken, *cidekarūpo* the consciousness of one form (#352). In this *sādhana* the *brahamajijñāsu* is *kṣāntiyuktah* (#356) and steadfastly endures the effort and the pain in reaching that *samadhi*, or perfect knowledge. For such a seeker attains a state of *dṛṣṭaduḥkheṣūanudvega*, (#422) nonchalance towards worldly sorrows. The question of the threefold suffering, *ādhyātimika*, *ādhidaivika* and *ādhibhautika*, does not arise, *prapanco vismṛtaprayah*, (#429) for he has forgotten the phenomenal world and his mind is *yasya cittam viniścintam.* (#431) devoid of anxiety. Śaṅkara, fully established in the Upaniṣadic Advaita Vedānta, thus sets out the diagnosis and prescription of *duḥkha* in this treatise and it is obvious that *duḥkha* in Vedānta is not ontic but epistemic.

Sri Aurobindo touches on the concept of *duḥkha* as envisaged by the Upaniṣadic *ṛṣi* when he talks of the difficulties of the mental being, the struggle between the "lower mental being which clings to the old egoistic way of seeing the world and reacting to its impacts"[3] and a higher and divine state. The mental being has a mentality that disfigures and distorts and is "the sport of a lower nature of pleasure and pain and dull neutral sensation incapable of its divine delight, (a) deformed knowledge and limping will incapable of sharing in or being in tune with that nature of Godhead".[4] The nature of mind according to Sri Aurobindo is that "it lives between half-lights and darkness, amid probabilities and possibilities, amid partly grasped aspects, amid incertitudes and half certitudes"[5] and despite this it strives to enlarge itself into the sunlight of gnosis. The human being at the mental level seeks the comfort and security of shadows of light rather than reach for the sunlit spaces of the higher mind. As Sri Aurobindo says:

> But man is a mental being and not yet a supramental being. It is by the mind that therefore he has to aim at knowledge and realise his being...Realised mental being and realised spiritual being are really two different planes in the arrangement of our existence...In their apparent nature the two are opposed; each is the reverse of the other. The divine is infinite and immortal being; the human is life limited

> in time and scope and form, life that is death attempting to become life that is immortality....The human is sensation of mind and body seeking for delight, but finding only pleasure, indifference and pain...The human is ignorance reaching out to knowledge by the comprehension of things in parts and parcel which it has to join clumsily together... the human found itself on separated multiplicity...between the two (the mental and the supra-mental) there are for the human being a veil and a lid which prevent the human not only from attaining but even from knowing the divine.[6]

While clearly recognising the pain of the human mind Sri Aurobindo rejects Śaṅkara's solution of negating one for the other. Not for Sri Aurobindo is the "dominant disgust of the world or an anti-vital indifference or aversion to the material existence."[7] For he says that "the mind may go from one to the other, rejecting one as it arrives at another and calling this the lower or that the higher existence. But to unify without losing, to integralise without rejecting, is its supreme difficulty."[8] The challenge and, therefore, the *duḥkha* of mankind, according to Sri Aurobindo, is to hold the two, the lower and the higher, the material and the spiritual, the human and the divine, in an integral whole, not in a somnolent *samādhi* but in a radiant and waking state. As he says "not only must the mind be able to rise in abnormal states out of itself into a higher consciousness, but its waking mentality also must be entirely spiritualised."[9] *Duḥkha* for Sri Aurobindo is the effort of rising into the higher and radiant planes of existence and yet at the same time living in the flickerings of the lower mind. Sri Aurobindo in enunciating *duḥkha* is clearly following the Tantric epistemology of *bhedābheda.*

The *smṛti* literature and the Rāmāyaṇa in particular gives its distinct colouration to the concept of *duḥkha.* The dominant emotion of the Rāmāyaṇa is *karuṇā* or pathos right from the anguished cry of the *kraūnca* bird till the end of the epic and within this *karuṇārasa* Rāma is shown as the epitom of perfection and is driven by an overwhelming sense of *dharma* that befits only an Āryan. Rāma's character shows his unflinching commitment to his duties of caste and family even at the cost of causing pain to those around him. If upholding *dharma* is the motivating force of various actions in the Rāmāyaṇa, *karma* is the underlying cause of events as they unfold, and thus it is that human suffering is given a cosmic dimension. "The epic rarely shows its heroes raising their eyes above the embroidery of the mysterious plan which guides their destiny...What happens in the present age, the *tretā yuga* is the mere unfolding of a divine plan wrought out in the *kṛta yuga*."[10] Such is the power of words spoken in the *kṛta yuga* that not only are they infallible but equally the consequences of those divine words must be endured with grace and dignity. This is the central message of the Rāmāyaṇa. Tiwari is right in pointing out that "Fidelity to man's spoken words, whatever the cost in terms of suffering, is looked upon as a reflection of the divine order."[11] Rāma's unquestioning adherence to the words of his father, and later even those of his subjects when he is king as he banishes Sītā, idealises the concept of upholding of *dharma*. It is the performance of one's duty according to *dharma*, notwithstanding any amount of suffering that it may bring, that offers redemption in the plan of the Rāmāyaṇa and elevates human suffering to a cosmic level. Rāma is more than a suffering hero in the Rāmāyaṇa, he becomes through his suffering the saviour of the universe.

Any discussion of Indian thought is incomplete without including a consideration of the Purāṇas. Amidst its many stories are hidden nuances of meanings and an entire system of knowledge and although they may lack the erudition of discursive thinking it touches the people of India in many different ways. Kept alive by classical and itinerant performing and visual artists alike, the message of the Purāṇas is ever present in the Indian mind. Although never far from metaphysical concerns the Purāṇas are grounded in earthly realities. The actions and accounts of mythic beings in the Purāṇas do not remain mere narrations but become a system of knowledge acquiring a special status of reality. From it, the people of India derive various values and norms, from it emerge various festivals and ceremonies, from it is the foundation of the *sāmpradayas* and thus it is that it forms the foundation of Hinduism. A common theme of the Purāṇas is that nothing that the world offers is satisfying or capable of bringing peace to the restless and anguished mind. Not only the obviously painful and unfavourable but also the pleasant and pleasing are experienced as binding and in the long run become sources of suffering. From among the older Purāṇas the Viṣṇu Purāṇa, offers important insight into the concept of Purāṇic suffering. A common theme of the Purāṇas is that suffering arises from indulging in sense objects, petty indulgences and lack of devotion. In a long and beautiful passage in the Viṣṇu Purāṇa this recurring theme is brought out:

> Whilst Kṛṣṇa and Rāma were thus sporting in Vraja the rainy season ended, the autumn appeared and the lotuses became full blown. The safari fish in their watery burrows were oppressed by the heat like a man by his selfish desires who is attached to his family. The peacocks, renouncing all amusements, became silent like the ascetics withdrawing themselves from worldly enjoyments considering their unreality. The clouds of shining whiteness, exhausted of their watery wealth, deserted the sky, like the wise who have acquired wisdom, departing from their homes. Evaporated by the rays of the autumnal sun, the lakes were dried up, like the hearts of men withered by the contact of selfishness. The silent waters of the autumn were beautified by white water lilies, like the minds of the pure by the perception of truth. The moon shone with undiminished brilliance in the sky crested with stars like the saint, who has reached the last stage of bodily existence in the company of the pious. The rivers and the lakes slowly went far off from their banks as the wise by degrees shrink from the selfish attachment that connects them with their wives and children. The swans again began to frequent those lakes which they had abandoned before like ascetics whose devotions are interrupted and they are again stricken with numberless afflictions. The ocean, with silent waters, became perfectly calm like the accomplished saint who has gone through rigid penances and has acquired undisturbed tranquillity of spirit.

> Everywhere the waters are as clear and pure as the minds of the wise who behold Viṣṇu in all things. The autumnal sky was perfectly free from clouds like the heart of the ascetic whose cares have been devoured by the fire of devotion. The moon allayed the fervours of the sun as discrimination removes the pain consequent upon egotism. The autumn removed the clouds from the sky; the muddiness of the earth and the discolouration of the waters, as abstraction draws away the senses from the objects of perception.[12]

The appeal of the Purāṇas was to the man on the street, the householder involved in the business of life who has neither the means nor the training to engage in philosophic discourse, the seeker who was influenced by the spoken rather than the written word and the devout for whom *bhakti* was the preferred route to knowledge. It saw the world as a snare for the senses, a trap for the unchastened mind, a mirage for uncontrolled desires and therefore *duḥkha* for it was to fall victim to the weaknesses of such a body and mind. Clearly its perception and therefore prescription for the alleviation of *duḥkha* was prosaic rather than poetic, practical rather than esoteric.

The Vedas had enjoined that Truth is one the wise call it by different names and thus it was that the historical period after the Vedas, for a thousand years and more, was marked by a fervent and fearless search for that truth. It was a time of great intellectual activity and advances, fervour and freedom. Ours was not a monolithic tradition, we were not bound by dogma or decree, we were not to follow a single messiah neither was the Hindu mind in its upward and godward ascent to be imprisoned within the pages of a single book or the cult of a single personality. It was a time of bold assertions, grand debates and a multitude of approaches to the problem and destiny of the human condition. Historically it was a period of socio-economic stability and the Hindu mind was not to be enslaved into a beaten track but rather was to soar in the vast and boundless sky of intellectual freedom and philosophic speculation. This was to produce a number of philosophic systems, the supremacy of the Vedas was to be challenged and even rejected by the heterodox philosophers, and the ambience was one of free and unfettered thinking. But freedom has its price and that was that a bewildering number of philosophic systems were developed, one contradicting the other. In particular the debate between *pravṛtti* or material activity and *nivṛtti* or cessation of activity was particularly discordant. Since activity is the defining feature of the human condition this disagreement was to lead to confusion in the mind of a seeker and hence produce a kind of *duḥkha*, understood now as ambivalence or confusion. This is the plight or *duḥkha* of Arjuna as portrayed in the Gītā. There is in the mind of Arjuna an ethical uncertainty, a certain loss of direction, an inability to decide whether or not to act. The dilemma for him is a normative one: what is the correct code of conduct for a Kṣatriya, to act in keeping with his innate nature or to go against it and cease from activity? The Gītā places this ethical dilemma in the context of the Mahābhārata war.

The Gītā, as we know it, is undoubtedly a later document in the Hindu tradition and certainly much later than the Mahābhārata. The consensus is that it was compiled around the 1st century BC, at a time when multiple philosophic systems had proliferated, one contradicting the other. It was a charged intellectual atmosphere with the dominance of the strongly Idealistic Upaniṣadic *nirvikalpa brahman.* There were raging debates as to the epistemic *bona fides* of the *savikalpa brahman,* a *brahman* that was cognised through the six senses. Śaṅkara had yet to appear on the Indian philosophic scene but already hints of the all too powerful concept of *māyā* or illusion were present. Buttressing the *nirvikalpa brahman* of the Upaniṣad, although in a different vein, was the *puruṣa* of the Sāṁkhya: solitary, somnolent, passive, detached, and quietistic, witnessing but uninvolved with the affairs of the world. The richly analytical system of Sāṁkhya, with its sharp division of *puruṣa* and *prakṛti,* is the bedrock of the Gītā and its majestic, atheistic and calm *puruṣa* overshadows Arjuna as he ponders his course of action. If Arjuna is to be inspired and driven by the vision of this *puruṣa* of the Sāṁkhya he must use his intellectual discrimination, desist from action, be uninvolved with the affairs of the world, care for his own personal *mokṣa* and retreat into a position of philosophical *nivṛtti* and engage in a yoga of inaction. But if this be the course of Arjuna's yoga what is to become of this *saṁsāra,* this world of multiple beings, a world defined and sustained by activity? Knowledge and action on the one hand and personal spiritual freedom and *lokasaṅgraha* or the welfare of the world at large on the other become contradictory if one is to be led by Sāṁkhya. This is the central problem of Arjuna and becomes his source of dilemma or *duḥkha.* It would be easy for Arjuna to attain his personal and individual *mokṣa* by a process of *jñāna* leading to *nivṛtti,* for he was after all a *yogī* and possessed by a radiant intelligence and discriminating knowledge. This was the way of Sāṁkhya and Arjuna could very easily become a consummate Sāṁkhya *yogī.*

Opposed to the passive and quietistic Sāṁkhya was the philosophic system of Yoga which emphasised knowledge through works. As Sri Aurobindo puts it so succinctly "The difficulty which Arjuna feels in understanding any possible synthesis of these oppositions is an indication of the hard line that was driven in between these two systems in the normal ideas of the time."[13] Yet another source of confusion for Arjuna was the opposition between Vedism and Vedanta, the *karmakāṇḍa* or ritual action advocated by the Veda and the *jnānakāṇda* or the lofty ideals of knowledge of the Upaniṣads. And, finally, another important source of dilemma for Arjuna is the opposition, that prevailed at the time of the Gītā, between personal spiritual freedom on the one hand and the welfare of the people at large, or *lokasaṅgraha,* on the other. While Sāṁkhya emphasised the former, Buddhism had through its doctrine of compassion and empathy, *karuṇā* and *metā,* underscored the need to be concerned with the world at large.

There was thus for Arjuna a tension between the Vedantic *mokṣa* and the Buddhist *nirvāna.* This was the central problem for the spiritual seeker at the time of the Gītā, a problem created by prevalence of multiple and opposing systems of philosophies without the lack of an integral and synthesising yoga. This was the very mandate of the Gītā, namely to formulate a yoga that would combine the best of the various systems and yet remain within the ambit and the spirit of Vedānta. The Gītā candidly admits that the scriptures are capable of creating bewilderment, confusion and delusion in the mind of the sincere seeker and sees the need to solve this problem. It achieves this formidable task by combining the language of the Sāṁkhya with the assertion of Vedānta and positing a third *puruṣa*, above and beyond the two *puruṣas*, the *puruṣottama*, which is the large and catholic repository of not only *jñāna* but equally *bhakti* and it is from this vast and radiant *puruṣottama* that flows the beautiful concept of dispassionate action or *niṣkāma karma*. The yoga of the Gītā dispels Arjuna's confusion and in so doing assumes a centrality as well popularity in the Indian tradition, and Sri Aurobindo reminds us that "it becomes a work of spiritual practicality, not of constrained religious and philosophical formulas and stereotyped dogmas."[14] The Gītā thus finds a practical solution to the delusion or the *duḥkha* of Arjuna.

When we come to the later Bhāgavata Purāṇa, composed around the 9th century, and the rich Kṛṣṇa Rādhā lore that flowed in the Indian tradition from then onwards, a tradition which included the Gītā Govinda and the prolific romantic literature in the *bhāṣās*, yet another type of suffering is enunciated, a suffering that was as intense as that of the Vedic and Upaniṣadic *ṛṣis* and the *viṣāda* of Arjuna in the Bhagavad Gītā, but had a human dimension to it, it was a suffering that was poetic and therefore revealed the human condition through a *rasa* and not through a doctrine, a suffering that bridged the gap between the sacred and the secular, and this was the suffering of the love torn Rādhā *virahiṇī*. *Śṛṅgāra rasa* has been discoursed upon right from Bharata, and romantic love has been the theme of countless artistic creations including Sanskrit court poetry, but romantic love acquires a different dimension, when after the Bhāgavata Purāṇa, the lovers were none other than Rādhā and Kṛṣṇa. When Kṛṣṇa performed the *rāsalīlā* in the enchanted forest of Brindavan on a full moon night of *śarad* the gopis danced in ecstasy and felt so possessive of Kṛṣṇa that each gopi claimed Kṛṣṇa as her own.

At this point in the *rāsalīlā* Kṛṣṇa disappears leaving the gopīs heart-broken longing for his return. This paradigm of *vipralambha*, or love in separation, then becomes the central motif of Kṛṣṇa poetry from Jayadeva to Kabir, a motif that highlights the intense longing between woman and man and especially between Rādhā and Kṛṣṇa, and becomes then an archetype of a unique type of suffering. Many and varied are descriptions of the love torn *nāyikā* longing for her beloved. Here are a few examples:

Averse from eating, turned from every object of the senses
and this too, that your eye is fixed in trance
your mind is single-pointed
and then this silence and all the world to you seems empty
tell me gentle friend, are you a *yogini* or *viyogini*? R̃asikapriyā.

Do not show me flowers for they seem like arrows
and as for garlands, keep them away for they are like snakes
do not wave a fan for their scented breeze maddens me
and do not rub sandal on me for it turns to fever
neither saffron for it burns
and give me not any betel for they are poison to me. Rasikapriyā.

Her peace of mind has vanished
and her body's splendour, which should increase each day, has gone
her appetite, her joy, her thirst,
her sleep are all forgotten. Rasikapriyā.

When will that day arrive when she will end my affliction
with the merriment of her sweet eye brows
will it ever be that she abides in my heart
with her camphor and musk like eyes as of a deer
and will that sweet moment dawn when she gazes on the lamp
and laughs and talks with me? Rasikapriyā.[15]

Tell me what to do
even the bed of water-drenched lotuses
dries up as he reclines
the coolness of sandal paste is no remedy
nor the hostile moon.
Be sure, O beautiful one
Kṛṣṇa pines away
from wanting you
day by day his body grows thin
his heart ignores all others
the doctors have left him without hope
his only medicine
the nectar of your lips. Vidyāpati.23[16]

Night has passed, may the day not pass by
the black bee has flown away
it is the age of the white duck
my little heart trembles
I do not know what my beloved will do to me
in the raw earthen pot water does not stay
the haṁsa has flown, the body fades away
from making crows fly again my arms are aching
says Kabir, my tale has come to an end. Kabir.[17]

The anguish of the *virahiṇī* so well described by poets and beautifully illustrated by miniature artists is vividly brought out by the poignant cry of birds such as *cakavī* and *papīhā*, birds that longingly cry out for their mate, an image used consistently by poets and especially by Kabir. In the cry of these birds is the anguish of separation, the pathos of loneliness, the pain of remembrance, the darkness of emptiness and the poignancy of longing born out of romantic love. While the poetic image of the suffering *virahiṇī* is striking, its metaphorical reference to the human soul longing for union with God is hard to miss. The reference to birds such as the haṁsa and the clay pot and the comparison of the *viyoginī* to a *yoginī* leave no doubt that the cry of the *virahiṇī* is to be read analogously with the outpouring of a devotee yearning for his Lord. Mishra is right when he says that "the essence of *bhakti rasa* must ultimately be discovered in this *alaukika* transfer in what was initially a mode of erotic separation."[18] The *virahiṇī* then is understood as the *ātman* longing for the *paramātman* and the poet, in keeping with the Indian poetic tradition, himself takes on the female persona. Whether or not one reads the anguish of the *virahiṇī* as an *ātman/parmātman* metaphor the pain of the *virahiṇī* by itself is portrayed with such an intensity and sincerity that it can stand on its own in the discourse of *duḥkha* or suffering in the Indian tradition.

The Gītā Govinda and other poetry in this genre while remaining in the *śṛṅgāra rasa* predominantly has unmistakable hints of *bhakti.* However as *bhakti rasa* gets a standing of its own it is expressed without an admixture of *śṛṅgāra* in the songs of Mīrā and other *bhakti* poets. *Bhakti* moves away from lofty monism to an earthly duality between man and God, a duality that can only be resolved through loving devotion to a personal God. For the *bhakta* pain or suffering takes on an ambivalent colouration within the dynamics of *bhakti* epistemology. On the one hand it is the separation of man and God that lets man enjoy the presence of the divine, but on the other hand it is this very separation that creates the pain and the longing for union with that divinity. *Duḥkha* understood in *bhakti* dynamics as separation between man and God, is therefore painfully sweet as the *bhakta* bridges that separation with ninefold activities, *navadhā bhakti.* This consists of *śravaṇam* rapt listening, *kīrtanam* chanting, *smaraṇam* fond remembrance, *pādasevanam* honorific touching of the feet, *arcanam* offering praise and homage, *vandanam* salutation and adoration, *dāsyam* service, *sakhyam* friendship and *ātmanivedanam* offering of one's innermost self.

A tradition's concept of *duḥkha* says more about it than its achievement and successes, its monuments and monarchs, for the true character of a civilisation, like that of a person, is revealed in what it considers painful. For pain, rather than pleasure, is a more primal and basic emotion. It is clear that the Indian tradition that we have briefly surveyed in this essay, does not regard pleasure and pain as antagonistic but rather complimentary, like the two banks of a river or the biune unity of *mithuna.*[19] Pain is not the opposite of pleasure, *sukha* not the negation of *duḥkha.* This is the real meaning of Buddha's affirmation *sarvaṁ duḥkham,* that all is suffering, implying that there should be no duality between pain and pleasure. To entertain a discourse of duality is to succumb to the trap of rationality. To a rationalist life evolves between pairs of opposites, light and dark, friend and foe, pleasure and pain, life and death. Traditional Indian thought from the Veda to the Gītā seeks the beauty and grandeur of spiritual and intuitive thought which rises above rational dualities and integralises polar opposites into a full and glorious whole. The concept of *pūrṇatva* or a serene and overflowing completeness, like a *pūrna kumbha,* which transcends rational opposites is a step towards *mokṣa* or spiritual freedom.

In early 20th century thinkers one detects a distinct shift in thinking about the concept of *duḥkha. Duḥkha* is removed from the metaphysical framework and is no longer understood as *avidya* or ignorance that hides us from knowledge, it is no longer relegated to the realm of spirituality but it is given a more material, this worldly dimension. *Duḥkha* in the 20th century whether physical, emotional, social or political was to be recognised and not considered an illusion, it had to be confronted and not escaped, it had to be resolved and not idealised, for it had a reality of its own and was not opposed to man's real nature. Ontic *duḥkha* for these thinkers was a fact of the human condition and had a reality of its own and to disregard it was to deny human emancipation. The *karma* doctrine, understood in its narrow sense, now recedes in the background and even though it is not denied, man takes charge of his destiny. In this group of thinkers are Vivekananda, Sri Aurobindo, Tagore, Tilak and Gandhi among many others. While being rooted in ancient tradition each of them reacted differently to the conditions that prevailed in early 20th century India. Vivekananda was appalled by India's poverty, Aurobindo by slavery to the British on the one hand and a forgetting of the Āryan heritage on the other, Tagore at the inability of the Indian mind to break out of the fetters of tradition and Tilak and Gandhi at the social and political conditions of the day brought on by the colonisers. *Mokṣa* for these thinkers was unthinkable unless *duḥkha* as they saw it was alleviated. They felt that it is in and through *duḥkha* that growth towards *mokṣa* is possible. The experience of *duḥkha* spurs the search for a state of perfection, for it is *duḥkha* that gives us a consciousness of our existence. There is in this attitude almost a befriending of suffering.

Tagore professes a religion of Man even as he affirms *ami kavi*, I am a poet. To suffer with dignity and yet go beyond it, according to Tagore, is the privilege of man and denied to the gods. For he says:

> Is there anywhere in the whole Universe such sacrifice? Such unconquered courage? Such fearless endurance? Such defiance of death? Towards what nameless, anguished shrine moves the triumphal journey seeking the end of suffering?[20]

Suffering, according to Tagore, does not make man a victim for "there is a fulfilment in love within the range of our limitations which accepts all suffering and yet rises above them."[21] Human individuality, Tagore insists, is both the source of suffering and a precondition of experiencing joy and love in the world. As long as he is able to feel joy and love in his relationship to the world he is prepared to accept suffering. Tagore's joy has room for pain, his concept of beauty a place for ugliness, his sense of eternality the fact of mortality, and his sense of *duḥkha* no room for despair.

> Beauty is sweet to us, because she dance to the same
> fleeting tune with our lives
> Knowledge is precious to us because we shall
> never have time to complete it
> All is done and finished in the eternal Heaven.
> But earth's flowers of illusion are kept eternally
> fresh by death
> Brother keep that in mind and rejoice.[22]

In moving towards a sense of joy and beauty, man, Tagore feels, expands his limited egocentric view of life.

> To the man who lives for an idea, for his country, for the good of humanity, life has an extensive meaning, and to that extent pain becomes less important to him.[23]

In expanding this consciousness man, according to Tagore, lives in greater harmony with the universe around him:

> The same stream of life that runs through my veins night and day runs through the world and dances in rhythmic measures. It is the same life that shoots in joy through the dust of the earth in numberless blades of grass and breaks into tumultuous waves of leaves and flowers.[24]

One clearly sees a movement in the 20th century thinking towards greater rationality, an acceptance of a mind that fragments rather than unifies. Fragmentation is a hallmark of rational thought for a rational mind delights in dividing, compartmentalising and drawing lines. For that rational mind it is either black or white, right or wrong, pleasure or pain. Time for that rational mind is always measured and space always bounded. This kind of rational thinking brings some superficial comfort for it creates order out of chaos, draws boundaries to enclose spaces of safety, measures time in a linearity that it understands and rejects circular time that it finds hard to fathom, looks for empirical certitude rather than dwelling on the uncertainty of dialectic, trusts perception rather than inference, is comfortable with the immediate rather than reach for the ultimate, prefers form to the formless. But rational thinking has its limitations for it imprisons the mind within narrow walls, tethers it to the ground instead of letting it soar and roam in the vast and boundless sky, finds a home within shadows of light rather than letting it bask in the brilliance of sunlit vistas, gives only a tentative nod to emotion and is unable to comprehend the majesty and grandeur of spiritual or intuitive thinking.

The different concepts of *duḥkha* presented so far represent various facets of Hindu Idealism where ultimate reality is spiritual rather than material, *nirvikalpa* rather than *savikalpa,* intuitive and inward rather than rational and intellectual, and for that Idealised mind *duḥkha* assumes an altogether different colour. Idealistic thinking thrives on holism and abhors fragmentation, seeks the serenity of spiritual silence rather than the noise of ratiocination. And into that spiritual silence is added the music and colour of the various arts. For this spirituality was not just an arid concept or a dry metaphysical thesis but acquired a reality of its own through the diverse and rich traditional arts, both classical and folk. Sacred literature and the world view it espoused was brought to life in ancient and medieval India by dance and drama, song and sculpture, by story tellers and itinerant performers, at fairs and festivals, in temples and courts. The ideas percolated deep into the psyche and became a part of the living truth.

Modernity for us in India and especially in urban environments meant a deprivation of the traditional arts as a meaningful part of life. Exposure to these arts, that once formed such an integral part of life, was only in auditoria and theatres. The modern urban mind having been impoverished from that rich and integral spiritual environment slips instead in ratiocinative activity and finds itself in a different ambience. It is an arid milieu when the mind operates with razor sharp intellectuality, when one question leads to another and endless questioning tires that mind into a state of fatigue and exhaustion. From this fatigued mind can arise only utter despair, it can only think in terms of cause and effect and will not accept the traditional concept of the *karma* doctrine, for it needs a reason for every event and turn that life offers. Such a mind ponders the immediacy of matter rather than the ultimacy of spirit, the problems of the here and now instead of the promise of the here after, the condition of the individual rather than consider the universal, it sits in judgement even in its limited view of the world and defines pleasure and pain as a child divides friend and foe. This is the condition of modernity, and it is in this ambience that the lofty concept of ancient *duḥkha* is transformed into modern emotion of despair.

ENDNOTES

1. Radhakrishnan, Indian Philosophy Volume 1, P.244. London: George, Allen and Unwin Ltd.,1966.

2. Swami Chinmayananda. Talks on Sankara's *Vivekacūḍāmaṇi.* Bombay. Central Chinmaya Mission Trust. 1974. The numbers that follow refer to the verses.
3. Sri Aurobiṇdo. The Synthesis of Yoga. p. 687. Pondicherry. Sri Aurobindo Ashram. 1976
4. ibid. p. 378.
5. ibid. p. 779.
6. ibid. p. 377.
7. ibid. p. 380.
8. ibid. p. 383.
9. ibid. p. 380.
10. Kapil N. Tiwari. Suffering: Indian Perspectives. pp. 120-121. Delhi. Motilal Banarasidass. 1986.
11. ibid. p. 122.
12. M.D. McLean. Suffering in the Purāṇas: The Visnu Purana, in Tiwari (Ed.) Suffering: Indian Perspectives. p. 178.
13. Sri Aurobindo. Essays on the Gītā. Pondicherry. Sri Aurobindo Ashram. p.75.
14. ibid. p. 103.
15. Free translation from Chapter 8 of Rasikapriyā of Keshavadasa.
16. W.G.Archer. (Ed.) Love Songs of Vidyapati. Delhi. Motilal Banarasidass. 1963.
17. A free translation of this Kabir *pada* from Kabir Granthavali quoted by Vijay C. Mishra in Suffering: Indian Perspectives. Kapil N. Tiwari (Ed.)
18. ibid. p. 244.
19. I am grateful to Dr. Kapila Vatsyayan for introducing me to this idea.
20. Rabindranath Tagore. Last Poems. Aurobindo Bose (trans.) London. MacMillan, 1952. p. 42.
21. Rabindranath Tagore. The Religion of Man. London, George Allen and Unwin. 1970. p. 126.
22. Rabindranath Tagore. Collected Poems and Plays of Rabindranath Tagore. Aurobindo Bose (tra.). London. George, Allen and Unwin. 1970. p. 295.
23. Rabindranath Tagore. Sadhana. London. MacMillan & Co. 1914. p. 49.
24. Rabindranath Tagore. Collected Poems and Plays. p. 33, 38.

4

ĀDI PURUṢA TO MĀNAVA, FROM PRIMAL MAN TO MANKIND

Harsha V. Dehejia

A scholar of modernity, as opposed to a scholar of antiquity, is faced with a dilemma. The antiquarian unearths or discovers objects and extrapolates from these objects the nature of the civilisation that created these objects. The modernist on the other hand, however, must contend with not only art objects of the period of history under study, but equally with a living civilisation made up of people and places, literature of different genres, organisations and institutions, spaces both sacred and secular, and recorded history from which these objects have arisen. The modernist must then decide whether to accept the verbal or written testimony of this living civilisation in order to come to an understanding of this period of history, or behave like the antiquarian and by-pass the people and institutions in favour of the art objects of that period. Our approach has been to choose the latter route and investigate and analyse the human image in modern Indian art in an attempt to come to an understanding of at least some aspects of modernity in India. We do this based on a firm conviction that good art, even more than literature, embodies the deepest feelings of the human psyche and provides a better reflection of the human condition than an empirical psycho-social probe. Creativity in the ethos of modernity cannot remain totally aloof from social realities of the day, and a deep understanding of what is created could be a mirror of the times in which it is created. Ranjit Hoskote is right in saying that:

> (art) experience gains significantly in depth when the viewer is also aware of the personal and historical circumstances

> in which these art-works were brought into being, the ideological, philosophical and formal concerns they reflect, the art historical moment in which they appeared.[1]

Carl Jung in a similar vein also states: "Consciously or unconsciously, the artist gives form to the nature and values of his time, which in their turn form him."[2] In undertaking this type of analysis it is important not to fall into the trap of personality cults or uneducated subjectivity,for an understanding and analysis of art, if properly carried out, should lead us to universal truths of the human condition, and away from superficial, trivial and unaesthetic details of the artist, the art object or the environment in which this art was created.

Any discourse about modernity presents several problems, and we in India have certain unique situations which change the dynamics of this type of discourse. The Indian tradition even from times prehistoric has never been a monolithic one, and at any given time there have been various and even divergent strands of thought as well as creativity. Thus, even in the heyday of the strongly Idealist Vedānta, we had the *nāstika* traditions such as the Buddhists and the Jains, not to mention the rationalist schools of philosophy like the Cārvāka and the Nyāya. It is not easy therefore in the Indian tradition to single out one system as representing the main stream or dominant thought, while relegating others to the fringes. This is in many ways the strength of the tradition. The same problem applies to modernity as well. In singling out one thread of thought or creative expression one cannot affirm that other opposing and divergent views and forms of creativity do not exist in the tradition. But at the same time, in our exploration of modernity, if one does find a stream or a thread, which appears different, one feels justified in not ignoring it, and indeed in exploring it further and wondering whether this perhaps is the defining feature of modernity itself.

A deep existential emotion of despair, not just psychological discontent, dejection, depression or disenchantment, is one such thread of the human condition of modernity in India, and one that is distinct from the eight primal emotions enunciated by

Bharata. A deep, epistemic, ontologic and existential despair has never been a feature of Indian thought and art, and we feel justified in exploring its emergence in modernity through the aegis of modern art. It is important at the outset to clarify that modernity should be understood and discoursed upon as a philosophical concept and not merely as a psycho-socio-historical evaluation of this period of the history of the Indian civilisation. This latter concept could best be described by the term modernisation, which brings in ideas such as Westernisation and would cover such problems as the effect of technology on human behaviour and institutions, and the state of family and social values under these forces. The definition of modernity offered by Lloyd and Susanne Rudolph though comprehensive is still largely psycho-social:

> Modernity assumes that local ties and parochial perspectives give way to universal commitment and cosmopolitan attitudes; that the truths of utility, calculation and science take precedence over those of the emotions, the sacred and the non-rational; that the individual rather than the group be the primary unit of society and politics; that the associations in which men live and work be based on choice not birth; that mastery rather than fatalism orient their attitude towards the material and human environment; that identity be chosen and achieved not ascribed and affirmed; that work be separated from family, residence and community in bureaucratic organisations; that manhood be delayed while youth prepares for its tasks and responsibilities; that age, even when it is prolonged surrender much of its authority to youth and men some of their to women; that mankind cease to live as races apart by recognising in society and politics its common humanity; that government cease to be a manifestation of powers beyond man and out of the reach of ordinary men by basing itself on participation, consent and public accountability.[3]

While not dismissing modernisation altogether as an unimportant concept, as it must remain an integral part of the study of modernity, modernity in its purest and essential sense must essentially remain a subject of study for the philosopher and not the sociologist, psychologist or historian. At the core of a philosopher's quest is the problem of understanding the human condition. Shanti Swarup is right in saying:

> Fundamentally, modernity necessitates subjecting all our ideas, social attitudes, values and belief systems and the methods and structures of production and action to rational critical inquiry in the light of current knowledge. It involves retaining, updating and improving upon what is valuable in tradition and rejecting what is untenable.[4]

Satchidananda brings in socio-economic factors when he defines modernity thus:

> Modernism emerged under different circumstances in different languages and often meant different things, though its common thrust was anti-romantic and meant an innovation of idiom that was essential to articulate the new perception of life in the context of industrialisation and urbanization.[5]

Most definitions of modernity dwell upon the many dimensions of social change, a change that is brought about by the transformation of traditionally directed societies. Defining modernity merely as the rejection and reversal of tradition is untenable for us in India, for surely the Indian ethos allows evolution within the folds of tradition. For us in India, tradition is not an encumbrance and does not have to be discarded if one has to progress. Andre Beatille is right in saying:

> "In science as in the arts tradition is kept alive by being subjected to continual scrutiny and renewal... One can work within a certain tradition and build one's work on it without being an advocate of tradition as such...The receptivity of a tradition to new elements from outside is an index of its health."[6]

He goes on to say that some cling to tradition for fear of modernity.

There are as many definitions of modernity as there are facets to it, for each discipline brings its own special view point. However it cannot be denied that for us in India modernity is closely tied with and inseparable from colonisation on the one hand and a post-colonial search for our identity on the other. We agree with Satchidananda when he says that "Modernism became a way of documenting the dehumanization of society in India after Independence with its attendant morbidity, alienation and loss of identity."[7]

The Indian tradition has in the past indeed explored rationalist systems of thought but it cannot be denied that the thrust of Indian thought has been arational, where rationality and ratiocination are accepted initially but eventually transcended. To an Indian philosopher therefore Indian modernity means unbridled and untethered rationality; a denial of philosophical Idealism in favour of Realism, it is the inability to bring to a stop, *nirodha,* the unceasing functioning of intellectuality and ratiocination, *cittavṛtti.* Stated differently it is the inability to undertake yoga. To use the metaphor of the Kaṭhopaniṣad the modern mind is "one which does not have understanding, a mind that is not constantly held firm, whose senses are uncontrolled, like the vicious horses of a chariot rider."[8]

It is the philosopher's job to probe not only *nāmarūpa,* or the outer material and objective world of name and form, and the psycho-social forces it is subjected to, but to penetrate the human psyche above and beyond it. A cornerstone of that probing is epistemology, for not only does it reveal the state of ultimate knowledge but the means through which it is obtained. The central concern for the philosopher is to seek an answer to the primal human question *ko ham,* who am I? It has been said *sarvaśāstraprayojanam ātmadarśanam,* the ultimate purpose of any inquiry is an understanding of the *atman* or the core of the human psyche. In other words the essential field of inquiry for the modernist should be epistemological, which brings him face to face with the central question as to the certitude or otherwise of knowledge and ultimate self-awareness, the means of acquiring that knowledge and the various creative expressions of that state of knowledge, or lack of it. The desire for knowledge is fundamental and a defining feature of the human condition. It is not only sought through different means or *pramāṇa* but subjectively experienced, and having experienced, is creatively expressed. Śiva expresses it through his *ānanda-tāṇḍava*, Viṣṇu through his *śayana* on the *ādiśeṣa* and Buddha expressed it through his enigmatic smile, Mahāvira through his wanderings as a teacher, the *bhakti* poets through their songs. Artists express that personal and subjective experience of knowledge through artistic expressions.

Art embodies the deepest emotions and innermost resonances of the human psyche and a study of the art of any period must lead us to an understanding of the psyche, individual or collective, of that period. This is the spirit of this inquiry, namely to investigate some selected aspects of modern Indian art and move from its *rūpa* to *arūpa*, from the surface and formal features of the art objects, especially in their depiction of the human form, to the spirit that it reflects, from its *sākṣādartha* to the *parokṣārtha*, from particular observations to universal truths that the art object embodies.

Modernity has both a chronological and ideological connotation. A chronological understanding of modernity denotes contemporaneousness and is therefore time bound and limits the scope of the inquiry to a certain period of history. Ideologically on the other hand, modernity implies a break in the collective psyche of the civilisation, an opposition to traditional structures of thought and feeling, and in this sense it must show how and why this rupture occurred, and whether any threads of continuity remain between the past and the present. The understanding of modernity, therefore, evolves between those two axes, that of chronology and epistemology.

Ideologically speaking, the term tradition for us in India is a loaded one and in the domain of philosophy generally refers to the classical *nigamic* and the *āgamic* streams of thought. The *nigamic* stream is represented by the Veda and the Upaniṣads and the various schools of philosophy that followed. In contrast to the *nigamic* or the classical stream the other is the non-Upaniṣadic stream represented by the *āgamic* schools of thought and art. And these two streams, the *nigamic* and the *āgamic*, continue to flow side by side, like the two banks of the river of Indian civilisation, at times syncretic and at others at variance with each other. The interaction between the *nigamic* and the *āgamic*, has been an on-going one. It is interesting to note that the *āgamic* stream incorporates many seminal ideas from the folk tradition and preserves it, and is in many ways responsible for maintaining the thread of continuity of the tradition. For whenever the *nigamic* tradition is interrupted it seems as if the *āgamic* tradition lends it an idea, a concept, a gesture and this seems to revive the *nigamic* stream that has survived, like the faded writing on a palimpsest.

The re-emergence of the folk ethos, in our arts, is an important part of the modernist movement for us in India. This nostalgic and historical recall of the folk ethos in the midst of modernity is considered by some to be the agenda of post-modernism. While post-modernism becomes a subject of independent study in the West, we in the Indian tradition must study modernity in tandem with post-modernism and cannot leave them in water tight compartments. And we do so for one main reason that is unique to India. While modernity was making its appearance in the Indian continent, mainly through colonisations, it did not embrace the entire population in its sweep as it did in the West. The march of modernity left behind large pockets, especially in rural India and middle class urban India, which were totally untouched by any of its aspects. It is these pockets, where time stood still, where tradition was unbroken and where the folk ethos remained alive and well, that became one of the well springs of the post-modernist manifestations for us in India. In many ways it is this folk stream that has been the subterranean stream of sustenance and nourishment in our art and thought.

It is important to note that the Vedic-Upaniṣadic period was aniconic and there is no evidence of plastic or visual art of the classical stream from that period, apart from the *vedi* or fire altar and *yūpa* or the pillar. The fire altar portrayed the cosmos through incorporating cosmic shapes such as the square, the circle and the triangle, but it was the pillar that was the main plastic manifestation of this period and which was to become the harbinger of later pillars such as the *dhvajastambhas* and the pillars of the *raṅgamaṇḍapa* of the temple and later the many iconic images of the classical tradition that followed. The pillar, though aniconic, played an important part in the Indian tradition in many different ways. Indra is said to have planted the first pillar of the universe. The pillar of Indra or *indrakīla*, separated heaven from the earth, and created a space where mankind could live and maintain a duality between them and the gods. It is important to recognise the creation of this duality as one of the primal steps in man's attempt at self-awareness, for there can be no awareness in a void.

The pillar, amongst other things stands for this epistemic duality, a duality that the *āgamas* emphasise and celebrate. The pillar also represents the *axis mundi* and takes us from the centre of the earth to the sky. It is common for the *sūtradhāra* of *nāṭya* to plant the *indrakīla*, the pillar of Indra, on the stage before the performance begins, thereby giving the stage a cosmic dimension and providing both the spectator and the actor with the all important inter-connection between the microcosm and the macrocosm. The *dhvajastambha* of the temple proclaims the same Vedic pillar and so does the *chatra* atop the stūpa. The *raṅgamaṇḍapa*, or the theatre of the temple, displays a multitude of pillars, creating that charmed space within the temple, where the senses can be indulged and affirmed. King Aśoka planted pillars to announce his conversion to Buddhism and it was this Aśoka pillar that was to become the insignia of modern India.

The pillar, though aniconic, was the first plastic representation of the Vedic *puruṣa*, as revealed in the *puruṣa sūkta* of the Ṛg Veda and represents our first concept of Man in space reaching out with out stretched arms, standing proudly erect, with his feet planted firmly on the ground and without any signs of fragmentation. The *puruṣa* or the Cosmic Man of Ṛg Veda had a thousand heads and a thousand eyes, such was his magnificence. No landscape would suffice for this primeval person as he stood proudly erect in the fullness and wonder of infinite space. But *puruṣa*, we are told by the Vedic *ṛṣi*, is greater than this, such is his splendour; all beings are a fourth of Him, three fourths lie in heaven. And the *puruṣa sūkta* ends with the powerful declaration: *vedāham etam puruṣam mahāntam ādityavarṇam,* I have known this mighty *puruṣa* refulgent as the sun.

In celebrating the *puruṣa* and in declaring that this *puruṣa* is to be contemplatively known, the epistemic hints of the anthropomorphic form and the space surrounding it in classical art can hardly be missed. Equally it gives the Indian artistic tradition its first canvas or artistic space or *kṣetra,* not merely a background or landscape, but a home as it were, where the human image will rest and reside and which will become the microcosmic representation of the macrocosm, where the infinite will be manifested through the finite, and where the cosmic *puruṣa* will be artistically placed. The artistic space hinted at in the *puruṣa sūkta* was an ordered one for it was a microcosmic representation of the macro-cosmos. The *sūkta* states that from the mind of the *puruṣa* arose the moon, and from his mouth were Indra and Agni born, from his navel came the mid-air, from his head the sky was fashioned, from his feet the earth and from his ears the quarters. Thus were formed the worlds. The limitless *puruṣa* was thus reduced to its finite form but could not be contained within that form, for the *puruṣa sūkta* says that such is his magnificence but *puruṣa* is greater than this.[9]

The concept of transcendence is a recurring and foundational one in the Indian artistic tradition. The cosmic *puruṣa* is reduced to its *saguṇa* and *savikalpa* form, a form that can be sensually perceived and enjoyed, but in doing so we are not denying at the same time its *nirguna* and *nirvikalpa* aspects. In seeking the security and stability of a visual or plastic form, the cosmic *puruṣa* does not abandon its desire and need and capacity for an infinite vastness, an ability to remain unfragmented, a certain timeless presence and a joyous transcendence. Such is the splendour of the *puruṣa* and equally so the quest of the human mind. Of equal importance is the fact that the Ṛg Veda, which is considered the first document of the classical Indian tradition, promotes and maintains a poetic ambience, where *kavya* is the prototypical art object. This poetic ambience, which created its transcendence and spirituality, was to form the foundation of the Indian artistic tradition, its *pratibhā* and inspiration, and remained so until modernity when arid rationality was to drive the creative energy more importantly than the poetic spirit.

While not denying the presence of rationalistic and even materialistic schools of philosophy in the ancient Indian philosophic tradition, the Indian artistic mind traditionally and prototypically is Idealistic or spiritual and seeks the wider and more beautiful vistas above arid rationality. While the cosmic *puruṣa* assumes a visual form but gives insistent hints of its formlessness, the Vedic *ṛṣi* in the *puruṣa sūkta* ensures that this magnificent form was to reside within a space that was ordered and which also gave ample hints of infinity. The aesthetic ethos of the Vedas was undeniably poetic. It was this cryptic and poetic definition of the artistic space that was to inspire the landscape of later mythic art. The *kṣetra,* or the artistic space of this *puruṣa,* was a replica of the cosmos and every inch of the space was well ordered with water being the foundation, followed by representations of earth, fire, wind and space at the very top within the defined space.

The concept of two levels of meanings in any verbal or plastic construct, an initial surface and another deeper, is already evident in the *puruṣa sūkta,* and forms the basis of the classical iconic tradition, with its rich symbol systems that was to follow. Our icons, like the *puruṣa,* had a surface appearance which was to be enjoyed on first impact but equally a deeper, hidden meaning which was to be understood and realised in quiet contemplation. The grand and erect *puruṣa,* standing tall in its dignity and majesty, a form which has to be celebrated through a thorough and proper understanding, is not only a concretisation of ultimate reality in a human form but equally stands for the certainty, stability and beauty of that reality. What is also implied in this *sūkta* is that the *puruṣa* thus conceived has to be known, understood, realised and not just ritually worshipped. All iconic forms in the classical Indian tradition owe their pedigree to the *puruṣa sūkta* of the Ṛg Veda and the concept of the human form and the space surrounding it that it celebrates. The human form from now on, in the Indian tradition, is endowed not only with effulgent beauty but equally with ultimate worth; it is to be an expression and embodiment of the beauty but equally the elegance and the certainty of *brahmajñāna* or ultimate knowledge, a knowledge that is the ultimate aspiration and within the grasp of mankind. The tradition emphasises in many different ways the strength and the beauty of ultimate reality expressed through the human form.

In spite of the grand and magnificent representation of the *puruṣa* in the *puruṣa sūkta* in the Ṛg Veda the psyche of the Vedic Indian had an inhibition for concertising ultimate reality in a plastic anthropomorphic form. Stated simply, the Vedic Indians refrained from making images. This, despite the fact that the *puruṣa sūkta* of the Ṛg Veda celebrates through the orality of poetry the *puruṣa* in a lavish anthropomorphic form. It is interesting to point out that, while the Vedas and Vedānta do not issue any definite proscriptions against the making of visible and palpable forms, there are strong hints at the inhibition of the Vedic tradition in making images. The Śvetāśvatara Upaniṣad clearly says, "there can be no image of him whose name is great glory."[10] The absence of images in the Vedic period has not been satisfactorily explained. Anthropologists have argued that since the Vedic civilisation was pastoral, the making and the transportation of images was clearly difficult and it is therefore that no images were made in that period. Sociologists put forth the view that since the Vedic culture was distinct and even at variance with the autochthonous or the folk culture, the making of images which was an important part of that indigenous culture, was on purpose shunned by the Vedic Indians to distinguish themselves from the natives.

Psychologists claim that the desire of the Vedic Indian to remain aniconic is in keeping with the elitist Vedic tradition of keeping sacred knowledge private and hierarchical and not offering it to the all and sundry in the population. While not rejecting any of these explanations the primary philosophic reason for the Vedic tradition remaining aniconic is the concept of the *nirguna brahman*, a concept that pervades the Vedas and the *Upaniṣads* and never totally leaves the Indian tradition. The central reason for the aniconic Vedic tradition therefore is epistemic, namely the recognition that ultimate reality is *nirguna* and *nirvikalpa*, devoid of attributes and beyond thought constructs, something that has to be spiritually experienced and not concretized or rationally discoursed, and it is this that explains the reluctance of the Vedic people to concertise ultimate reality into a form.

Indian philosophy is the story of the tension between the *nirguṇa* and the *saguṇa brahaman*, and *nirvikalpa* and *savikalpa jñāna*, a tension that not only determines the religious culture of its proponents and adherents but equally has a direct bearing on the creation and celebration of images. Dadu put it beautifully when he said:

> Incense craves to dissolve itself into fragrance and fragrance wants to remain enveloped in incense. Melody seems to find itself articulated in rhythm and rhythm wants to get back to melody. Idea craves to be embodied in form and form seems to release itself in idea. The limitless seeks its intimate association with the limited, and the limited craves to lose itself in the limitless. I know not whose logic it is in creation and destruction, that there is an unceasing intercourse after freedom and freedom is always looking for a nest in bondage.[11]

While the *nirguna* school asserts the ultimacy of the formless, the *saguṇavadins* posit beauty and meaning in form, a form that can be sensually celebrated. While the *advaita* Vedantins consider form to be a definite hindrance, the *viśiṣṭādvaita* theology regards form as meaningful only so long as it is considered to be a part of the body of God, while for the *āgamavādins* such as *Kāshmīr Śaivites*, form is the very doorway to the formless. Form is not only visual but equally verbal, and what can be said about visual and palpable images derives from the discourse about the strength or limitation of language to grasp ultimate reality. In fact the discourse about the bonafides of form starts with an examination of language, its strengths and limitations. The Upaniṣadic declaration: *yato vāco nivartante aprapyo manasā saha*, where the words return baffled. unable to grasp ultimate reality, summarises the hesitancy of the *ṛṣis* of yore to trust language with the task of grasping or expressing ultimate reality. Equally the vivid exchange between the master and the student in the Chāndogya Upaniṣad where the master asks the student to open a fruit to ultimately reveal the emptiness within the fruit, leads to the conclusion that "it is from that emptiness that this magnificent peepal tree has grown."[12] While the Vedas hint at the limitation of language and therefore images, the Upaniṣad leaves no doubt about its strongly Idealistic position.

Another important feature of this early period of the Indian tradition was that it was joyous and optimistic in its world view and outlook. Mankind was promised *mokṣa,* the certitude of knowledge was asserted, and the outlook was never apocryphal. Tied with the concept of *mokṣa* was the pan-Indian idea of *karma,* understood as cosmic justice. While *karma* as a doctrine can have many shades of meanings, the one important concept of *karma* is that ultimate and cosmic justice is never denied. The just rewards for meritorious acts are to be eventually obtained if not in this birth, in the next. And by the same token, there is a reason and an explanation from acts of the previous births for the misfortunes and miseries of this birth. The strength of the *karma* doctrine, at all levels, is that it does not allow any despondency or existential absurdity to creep into the human condition. It is important to state this foundational premise of Indian thought, even though it is obvious, because some aspects of modernity would question this concept, and in turn this would affect the creative expression of the human image in the hands of the modern artist.

Although the folk tradition were prolific image makers and folk images are therefore pre-historic it, was not until the Purāṇic period of the Indian civilisation that the familiar and well loved images in the classical Indian tradition burst forth, images of Viṣṇu, Śiva and Śakti, and a plethora of other images that were to dominate Indian art and thought for almost two millennia, and those images are still with us. Although the hold of the Vedas and its exegetes had weakened, the *puruṣa sūkta* remained the fountainhead of inspiration for the Purāṇic mythic images. So important are these Purāṇic images that it would not be wrong to say that classical Indian visual art and Purāṇic images become synonymous; one could not think of one without the other. The cosmic *puruṣa* of the Ṛg Veda was transformed into the many and varied mythic images of the Purānas. The Purānas also led to the development of sectarian Hinduism or the *sampradāyas.* These Purāṇic images therefore became cult images and were the centre of a variety of bhakti ritual practices of the *sampradāyas.*

The basis of these Purāṇic images was myth and myth is so central and foundational to the classical Indian tradition that we do not even have a Sanskrit word for myth; *gāthās* and *kathās*, our songs and stories, is the nearest that we can come to, to represent the idea of myth in Sanskrit. Myth was high and cosmic drama and covered the gamut of emotions from *śṛṅgāra* to *bībhasta* and *hāsya* to *raudra*, all eight *rasas* as enunciated by Bharata. It was Abhinavagupta who added the ninth or *śānta rasa* and it has been rightly said that this *rasa* was a contribution of the Buddhists and in turn becomes the defining feature of Mahāyāna Buddhist images. The root of myth was *pratibhā* or creative imagination and this was the fountainhead of all the Purāṇic stories and the various artistic images it inspired. For these mythic beings were not historical persons but were born out of the fertile and radiant imagination of our *ādikavis* and *ādiśilpīs*, our first poets and story tellers, and which stories were passed on later to our pristine sculptors and painters. Our culture and our images are stored in our stories and not in our doctrines. It is important to note that *pratibhā* which is the seed of myth arises from *dhyāna*, which is contemplative, meditative, creative imagination and not rational thinking or ratiocination.

Mythopoesis that arose from this *pratibhā* required that the mind be elevated, that the artist in his *dhyāna* rise from the manas to the *manaso manaḥ*, the mind of the mind, a state of radiant, non-cognitive awareness. The mind is lifted from the immediate world around the artist, a world characterised by psycho-social forces, volitional activities, a mind that oscillates between the dualities of pleasure and pain and is driven by the intellect. It is when the mind is elevated from this time and space bound world, it is when the mind transcends the particular to envision the universal, that *dhyāna* arises, and it is in this state of *dhyāna* that myth is born and cosmic events are translated into human terms, and the cosmic *puruṣa* acquires a human form, whether it be *samudra manthana*, or Siva-Pārvatī *vivāha* or the killing of Mahiṣa or the tender love of the gopīs in Brindavaṇa and a thousand other mythic situations. Myth is not only a source of our classical images but equally forms a system of verbal and visual knowledge.

Dhyana for the Indian artist was a disciplined activity and one that could be deliberately induced. This *dhyāna* of the artist is not a trance, in the sense of loss of volitional control, or a content-less ecstasy, but a meditative discipline focussed on the cosmic *puruṣa* with the express purpose of revealing its form. The artist sees the form of the cosmic *puruṣa* in his *dhyāna* just as the Vedic *ṛṣis* hear the cosmic sounds out of which they compose the hymns. The desire on the part of the sage-artist to visualise the cosmic *puruṣa* is the key to the entire *dhyāna* and underpins the transformation of a personal, intellectual experience to a larger, universal vision. The sage artist adores and delights in the form that arises in his mind. This could be called an inner or aesthetic adoration in contradistinction to the ritual worship that is performed by a devotee. On the basis of the sources available to him, Mulk Raj Anand describes the artist's *dhyāna* thus:

> The artist performs purificatory ablutions and sits down to focus his attention on ... a *dhyāna mantra.* He then offers flowers, incense and other gifts to the form conceived. The mental picture is thus seen in all its details and the work of art is complete in the mind even before being translated into form. The artist then begins the task of technical elaboration, during which time he must hold fast to the conception evolved through yoga... The kind of mental state designed to be secured through the practice of yoga can also be cultivated by the artist through tuning up the functions of the body and the mind into perfect obedience

to the faculty of intuition and through deliberate invocation of dreams..."[13]

It is important to understand the dynamics of myth and its creation into a visual form through *dhyāṇa* to understand traditional art, for an important feature of modernity, as we shall see later, is its breaking away from myth and therefore from *dhyāna*. This *dhyāna* of the traditional artists broke away from the limitations of time and space, tore away from the personal to the universal, from intellectuality to intuitive feeling, from the duality of subject and object, from the limited perspective of cause and effect and from chaos to serenity. Within this meditative and mystical *dhyāna* not only were images visualised but emotions associated with that image were experienced by the artist. It is from this beautiful *dhyāna*, where the mind rose above the questioning, fragmenting intellect that the basic eight emotions enunciated by Bharata arose. It becomes clear why Bharata treats the emotional states as primal and beautiful and does not need to either defend or explain them. The soil from which modern emotions arise and are experienced by the artist and then artistically expressed is very different from that state of *dhyāna* and we moderns, artists and aesthetes alike, therefore need to treat modern emotions differently.

Mythopoesis in the Indian tradition came to an end around the 10th century and the Bhāgavata Purāṇa was one of the last Puranas to be conceived. Even though no new myths were added to the Indian storehouse after the 10th century, the Indian mind was seized by *bhakti* and it was this that propelled and kept alive the multitude of mythic images, and continues to do so even today. *Bhakti* not only legitimised the various mythic images in many different ways but equally upheld the optimistic outlook on life. *Mokṣa* understood as spiritual freedom, or perfect knowledge, was promised to the *bhakta* and there was no question of entertaining any form of despair within the *bhakti* world-view. God for the *bhakta* was not only omnipotent and omniscient but equally just and compassionate. *Bhakti* further was the main driving force of the building of temples and providing a home for the various mythic images. The temple created a sacred space not only for the cult image in the sanctum but equally for the large number of images, sacred and secular, both inside and outside it, and created an ambience where these images were worshipped and venerated and celebrated in many different ways. Mythic art which was mainly sculptural, did not stand alone, like a picture in a gallery, but was in an organic relationship and resonated with other sculpted images in the temple, to make the temple itself a holistic piece of art.

Along with the religious and aesthetic aspects of the temple were socio-political considerations of equal importance. A temple was a public place and temple art was therefore monumental art. This needed the endowment by royal or noble patronage, principally for economic reasons, and the art therefore became an expression of the power and world view of the individual king and the dynasty at large. There was a coming together of the sacred and the secular, this worldly and other worldly considerations, in the construction and celebration of the temple and its multiple images. No king, while presiding over his *prajā*, would allow an artistic expression of existential despair in the temple. To do so would not only be sacrilegious but be tantamount to abdicating responsibility and accepting defeat on the part of the king and his dynasty, for the king was not only the worldly representative of divinity but at the same time the secular head of the kingdom. The large number of secular images in the temple were also essentially joyous and celebratory, whether it were the sensuous *madanikas* or playful *kinnaras* or obedient courtiers. And lastly, ancient Indian art was not the product of an individual but a group of artists who shared a common lineage, worked with shared symbols and functioned in *shrenis* or guilds. In sharing artistic creativity, whether it was with other members of the family or the larger community of artists within which he worked, the artist was not in a world of his own but in a world of shared ideas and sensibilities and a universal vision. All this was to change with the onset of modernity in India and have an effect on the human form in modern Indian art.

The turning point in the Indian artistic tradition, mainly in urban India, came with India's colonisation. It has been said that nothing drained and altered the Indian psyche more than the European colonisation of India. While the Hindu psyche had dealt with the Buddhists and the Jains, and had encountered the Muslims in a variety of ways, it was the white European who was to create a sense of self-doubt, uncertainty and insecurity in the mind of the modern Hindu. Nirmal Verma correctly states that "Indians had already built up such a self-contained, sophisticated metaphysical system, which answered all their needs and enquiries that they had nothing more or new or important to learn from the others."[14] The European brought with him not only the arrogance of the conqueror but more importantly subjected the Idealistic and mythopoeic Indian mind to the onslaught and aridity of rationality. European rationality rests on the shoulders of the trinity of Descartes, Freud and Marx, who pursued rationality each in their own unique way and caused a fragmentation rather than an assimilation, a rupture rather than a healing, of the human psyche. The quintessential Indian mind, given as it was to intuitive and mystical thought, had upheld myth in many different ways, through religion and the arts, through culture and values.

The European colonisers were unable to deal with a mythopoeic civilisation and its underlying vision. To them the mythic world view was irrational not arational, mythic beings were monsters and not icons, mythic art was without any aesthetic merit and the worship of these images was sheer idolatry. Verma is right in pointing out that "The network of beliefs, myths and rituals, which provided a continuous cultural and spiritual nourishment to millions of Indians was not only not seen by the white man, but he firmly believed that it did not exist."[15] The case of the Didarganj *yakṣī* illustrates this attitude. Recovered from the river this ancient *yakṣī* led to adoration and worship by the natives while the British administrators thought it fit to display it in a museum. Unable to respond to Indian aesthetics these Europeans were incapable to move from the outer form of these images to the formless spirit they embodied and therefore were inept to come to even a tentative understanding of them. It was this

Orientalist attitude on part of the British that was to lead to a schism between the visual and the performing arts in modern India. For when it came to classical dance and music, the Europeans neither understood nor cared about that art form, and it was for this reason that the performing arts were left untouched and unaltered and allowed to flourish in their own milieu and continue their *paramparā* and do so even today.

Equally untouched by the European, who had little use or understanding of it, was what Haku Shah calls village ritual art. Dismissed by Western art historians as *desī*, folk, little art, or craft, this art form has come once again into the mainstream and forms a part of the post-modern artistic movement for us in India. Folk art survives even today, unspoilt and yet open to new influences, and has refused to fall prey to what I will argue as urban intellectual despair. While it is not necessary or possible to explore this art in any great detail in this essay, it is important to note some of its main features, features that have protected it from the ravages of modernity. Village ritual art is both spontaneous on the one hand but needs the discipline of generations of skill on the other, and has a certain life and vitality of its own. While their materials such as terracota or clay or fibre are organic rather than synthetic, even their tools can be seen as art objects and the more the tools are used the more lively they get.

In creating such rural art objects many other arts serve to make the art object grow and give life to the main work. For example when the tribals of Gujarat paint Pithora, the painting is accompanied by singing, drumming, dancing, trance and the sacrifice of animals. And finally the celebration and enjoyment of Pithora requires the lighting of lamps and the sound and the rhythm of music and dance. These arts are truly called the living arts of India. The stark contrast between this and the sanitised staring by an onlooker at a piece of modern art on the walls of a gallery is only too obvious. In the sterile ambience of an art gallery or a museum there is no interaction between the artist and the aesthete, no possibility of a dialogue, no oral discourse or debate, just a blank staring, not the serene contemplative solitude of a temple, or the joyous celebration by the people, but the lonely alienation of a modern art space, all of which only serves to increase the starkness of the artistic encounter and enhance the feeling of despair both in the artist and the aesthete.

The distancing by European colonisers from the performing arts and village ritual arts, left these arts untouched by the onslaught of modernity, but when it came to the visual arts, mainly painting, the colonisers influenced Indian painters in many different ways, an influence that was to change not only the Indian creative mind but its artistic expressions significantly. The Europeans felt that modern India should break with its past, an event, as Verma correctly points out that had never taken place in "India's psyche not even under the most intolerant Islamic rulers."[16] Verma goes on to say that:

> Europe's colonisation of India was not merely confined to some territorial space but went much further and deeper; it sought to colonise India's sense of time, its present being merely a corruption of the past; its past,though glorious, believed to be dead and gone.[17]

Verma rightly latches on to a statement ascribed to a Bengali journal at the turn of the century which described itself as an organ of the people who were "Hindu by birth and yet European by education" and then goes on to say:

> The small, apparently cynical dictum of a magazine perhaps most lucidly sums up the position of the liberal westernised Hindus who were in the forefront of the so-called resurgence movement in India. It was a position of increasing accommodation and assimilation of the humanist ideals of European civilisation. To be Europeanised by education essentially implied acceptance of the historical idea of progress which established Europe as the vanguard in the field of knowledge and enlightenment. From this position, it was just a small step to accept the self image of Europe as the ideal image of man himself. It was but logical that this would lead the Hindus - at least the most enlightened of them - to radically revise their traditional conception of

> the self. It ceased to be, what it had always been in the past, a part of a larger reality, *atman,* as a mirror-image of *parmatman,* a microcosm within a macrocosm. The idealised image of the European man subverted the Hindu image of his own self reducing it to a state of 'sub-self', a minor accessory to a larger reality, not of *brahman,* but of the Spirit of History moving across the earth through centuries to seek its ultimate fulfilment in the European man.[18]

Verma's concept of the subversion of the self by European education lays the ground for the fragmentation of the self, as expressed by modern Indian artists, that we shall be alluding to as the essay progresses.

While the subversion of the Indian mind, particularly of the urban intellectual, under the onslaught of colonisation is accepted without a debate, what is also important to note is that in the first fifty years of Independence a variety of social and political forces have been unleashed which has affected the Indian sensibility even more. After the first few heady years of nascent freedom there has been a *manthana,* a churning of the Indian psyche, a churning that has released vicious poisons and has taken away the radiance and the glow of that ancient spirituality and freshness. Kṛiṣṇa Iyer sums up the mood of post-colonial India when he writes:

> I write these pages in anguish because I find that everything that India stood for is in grave peril of subversion. Adi Shankara is in near oblivion...We are in crisis of the spirit and in material achievements. Our values are under assail. Our unity is breaking up. Our rich diversity is being regarded as a mere syndrome, while in truth it is our precious pluralistic tradition, and the wonder of the Indian microcosm that is being virtually wasted by simian cultural imitation, moral miasma and material degradation. The disease of affluenza and sensually corrupt consumerism is flourishing as negative counter-culture, annihilating universal compassion. The new gods incarnated as multinational corporations, narcotic terrorism and underworld plunder are afflict-

> ing and overpowering us. Death and darkness are conquering life and light.[19]

The malaise of modern post-colonial India is a complex phenomenon, with multiple layers of cause and effect, and cannot detain us in our investigation of the modern emotion of despair. Suffice it say that had the web of social and economic forces played out differently it is entirely possible that we would have found our ancient spark of enlightenment again. But the fact remains that the reaction of the urban intellectual to the stresses of post-colonial India stem from the same basic rationality that we learnt from the colonial masters. The litany of problems of post-colonial and present day India cannot be ignored or brushed away, they are daunting and challenging, but to succumb to a state of cynicism or despair because of them speaks of a mind that has lost its ancient habit of remaining radiant and unperturbed, for it is a modern mind that engages in a knee-jerk reaction to events and circumstances, it is a homeless mind that is carried away by the flood of socio-economic adversities and moral and ethical dilemmas, it is an uncertain mind that questions the certitude of ultimate or perfect knowledge.

In investigating modernity in our visual arts there are a number of strands that might demand our attention, for the entire question of modernity is complex, multi-faceted and multi-factorial. In particular, modernity in India is tied with the question of Orientalism and Nationalism, two factors that are intertwined with the expression of modernity in our visual arts. Our inquiry, while accepting the effects of these two currents, will not directly address itself to it, but will inquire into the emergence and expressions of despair in the psyche of the modern urban Indian artist.

The traditional Indian artist of the 17th and 18th century India who had valued and preserved hoary but dying norms of Indian art, was being slowly transformed into the modern Indian artist in the Raj. Not only were our artists encouraged to copy European techniques of painting but more importantly they acquired the European mind-set which thrived in urban spaces and encouraged individuality and upheld rationality. The rural or traditional

Indian artist, whether a potter or a painter, living within a community, creating and re-creating mythic forms did not quite fit into the European ambience which the Raj ushered in. The first generation of modern Indian urban artists of British India vied for the same recognition as their European peers. It was in Calcutta in 1854 that the Government School of Art was opened and it soon became a focal point for modern Bengali artists. The School was the starting point of not only a new aesthetic but equally a new sociology in modern India's visual art. While many modern Indian artists were patronised merely to produce images of the natives, which the British could carry back home as objects of curiosity, others started doing portraits, landscapes, book illustrations and engravings, an art form that suited mainly the British as well as the *bhadraloka* or the Westernised Bengali middle class taste. Creativity in these artists was replaced by a slavish imitation, the ability to portray a mythic vision was instead supplanted by the ability to paint reality as it is, mythopoesis was replaced by *yathārthavāda*, seeing at it really is. The Indian artistic mind was being taught to abandon its penchant for mystical transcendence but relish instead realism and rationality. Late 19th century realism for the Indian artist was an odd mixture of nationalism and nostalgia, but equally it was an attempt to adapt to Western ideals of rationality in native terms. The 19th century Indian urban realist wavered from a dim attachment to ancient myth on the one hand and a flickering attempt to Westernise his format on the other. Anand is right in saying that

> " The British quick on the heels of the Minto-Morley Reforms, had hit upon an art policy for India and included oriental art as part of the curriculum at the school. This brought on the scene bad imitations of what one critic has called decadent Moghals, degenerate Rajputs and defunct Ajanta."[20]

The modern Indian artist groomed in the Calcutta School, and in the name of Oriental art, substituted mundane creativity and rationality for the visionary *pratibhā* of our ancient artists. Indian art of this period, while possessing an outer Indian content lacked a certain inner Indianness. For neither the nautch girl, nor a

Hindoo pilgrim, nor the Indian dhobi and other paintings of this ilk contained any real emotive content, or *rasa,* which is the hallmark of traditional Indian art. The "figures of (this art) were reduced to a certain native stereotype with a set dark-skinned appearance and static poise reserved for the Indian lower orders."[21] The Calcutta School of Art rapidly changed the urban middle class art scene. Not only were artistic expressions undergoing a change but equally the sociology and patronage of art was witnessing a transformation as well. High art was visual art, namely painting, and was no longer mythic or monumental art, but it was urban art with realistic themes and its patrons were not the nobility and the royalty but the upper and middle class Bengalis. With the entire artistic ethos undergoing such a change it is not hard to expect that the artistic expression of the human form in the hands and brushes of urban artists was to change as well. The majestic cosmic *puruṣa* of the tradition was replaced by earth-bound man. Those artists who were displaced by the disappearance of the Nawabi culture of courts such as that at Murshidabad, and who were the last remnants of traditional artists of mediaeval India, and who were not privileged to belong to the School, also flourished in this urban ambience of Calcutta and produced what has come to be called bazar art. These included the Kalighat painters and the metal engravers at the Bengali presses at Bat-tala. Guha-Thakurta is right when she says that

> "by the new parameters set by Anglo-Indian art, picture production at Kalighat and Bat-tala stood clearly demarcated as native and traditional with an inherited pool of images, conventions and clientele"[22]

Despite the British influence the Kalighat artists, who traced their lineage to the *patua* painters, brought a distinct, albeit folkish, Indianness into their paintings. Not only did they draw from the store of mythological figures for their inspiration but also portrayed satirically the foibles and emptiness of Bengali middle class society of the time. These Kalighat artists while remaining under the influence of the Raj, broke new ground in reflecting social reality through their paintings. For the first time for us in India, man as artist was confronting man as a social entity and it was this that produced Indian realism of the late 19th century. In doing so they worked within the stronger literary tradition prevalent at that time "with its strong currents of humour and irreverence that flourished in the popular songs, *jatras* and song performances of Calcutta."[23] Thus the Kalighat painters took up the Elokeshi episode and exposed every aspect of this scandal. In the hands of the Kalighat painters the *nāyaka* and *nāyika* of mediaeval India were replaced by the Bengali *babu* and the rapacious courtesan. It would not be wrong to say that in the art of the Kalighat painters was the first sustained Indian artistic expression of the alienation of the traditional Indian from the Westernised urban society of modern India. There was disenchantment and satire in this art but there was no despair in an existential sense, for the Kalighat painters were after all, devotees of Kali. While establishing new norms in the content of modern Indian painting Kalighat painters were also pioneers in their technique, replacing paper for cloth and water colours in place of the traditional tempera or gouache. It is important to take note of Kalighat paintings for a proper understanding of modern Indian art, for not only did they hold sway for almost a century at a pivotal time in the aesthetic history of modern India but also provided the bridge from traditional to modern art. The human image in their hands was no longer the source and expression of effulgent beauty and of ultimate reality but of the mundane and social reality of the 19th century Indian. The Kalighat paintings were indeed a turning point in the modern visual Indian artistic tradition.

At the turn of the 20th century a number of artistic currents were flowing in Bengal which came together to form what is called the Bengal school. Besides the Kalighat painters there were the revivalists like E.B.Havel, Ananda Coomoraswamy, Sri Aurobindo and Sister Nivedita who sought to revive traditional art. This revivalism was intertwined with the strong and effervescent nationalism in Bengal. Here is a clear example of the forces of modernity and post-modernism working in tandem in the late 19th and early 20th century urban India. The murals of Nandalal Bose for the pandal of the Haripura meeting of the Indian National Congress is one of many examples of this genre of art. An artist, who was not from Bengal, but who cannot be missed in this axial period of modernity is Ravi Verma. Ravi Verma drew upon traditional mythology, mixed it with Western techniques and produced images which had wide spread popular appeal. In his hands there was this uneasy coming together of the mythical and the realistic and served at once the purpose of "European Orientalism and Indian nationalism".[24] The Indian mind was like the two faced Janus, looking back and forward, claiming the past and staking the future. Ravi Verma's art "grew to be a highly popular and widely circulated brand of Indian art, cutting across the divide between artists and artisans and between elite and popular tastes in pictures."[25] Ravi Verma has been denigrated in recent times but it is not important for us to pass artistic judgement on his art, or any other art for that matter, for that is not our mandate. Our concern is to see how the urban Indian psyche was reacting to the winds of modernity that were blowing in 19th century India and what it did to the depiction of the human image in modern visual art. Satchidananda is right when he says that:

> The city has been a metaphor for all that is modern and modernism itself has been more or less an urban form of art, both in India and abroad...It is here that artists have experienced that modern phenomenon called alienation, that paradoxical position of independence coupled with social indeterminacy. Cities...have always been places of conflict, transformation and novel consciousness that stimulate cultural innovation along with a feeling of moral and communicative crisis.[26]

Between the Revivalists on the one hand and the Ravi Vermas on the other lay yet a third and powerful stream of artistic thought and this was epitomised by the Tagore family. Despite, or probably because of, the emergence of modern Indian art of the 19th century, Rabindranath Tagore was restless and felt that the Indian artist was ossified. He "became the catalytic agent of change, not only motivating and inspiring Gagan, Aban and Nandalal to break away from traditional structures of art but bringing new vitality and life through shaping new styles and forms."[27] There was the strong urge and need to break away from the opposing trends of Revivalism on the one hand and the Ravi Verma brand of Indianness on the other, to be Indian in a uniquely modern way, to be intellectual rather than sentimental, be rational rather than emotional, be modern rather than romantic. Tagore fostered modernity in his paintings while retaining traditional sentimentality in his poetry.

In the midst of the many winds of change we must not lose sight of our main focus and that is the human image and its transformation in modern Indian painting. The jolt that Rabindranath gave the Revivalists led to a radical remaking of the human form in Indian visual art. Thus far Indian visual art was tied mainly to mythic and as well to secular literature on one hand and to dance on the other. It is important to note that this corpus of literature and the tradition of dance was the bedrock from which the various visual forms were to emerge. As Kapila Vātsyāyana rightly points out "in the (ancient) aesthetic world there was an unchallenged acceptance of the primacy of literature. All other arts were perhaps only illustrations of the content of literary pieces."[28] A similar sentiment is echoed by Devangana Desai when she says, "Without a knowledge of Sanskrit literary conventions I could not have gone beyond a stylistic analysis of Khajuraho. Literature sensitised my eyes to the layered, rhetorical story-tellers and architecture we find there."[29] The modern Indian aesthete saw the emergence of modern literature and the link between *sāhitya* and *śilpa* or literature and the visual arts was lost and each was to forge its unique identity. The two parted company and both in their own right became the artistic vehicle of the urban artist.

Satchidanand regards Ghalib as our first modern poet and it is interesting that Ghalib expresses that state of alienation and fragmentation in his poetry. Satchidananda writes:

> Ghalib is one of the first masters to bring about that radical transformation in the nature of lyric that is typical of modernism. He very often abandons the traditional position of the lyric poet as the lover, the courtier, the patriot and the sage. The aspiration for an inaccessible order, a feeling of doubt, disbelief in the divine promise, the possibility of error, confession of sin, meanness and misfortune: all these characteristics of the modern lyric are discernible in Ghalib's verses...and the lyric that expresses a transitory mood or a momentary illusion seems apt and relevant...the surface of language seems to grow opaque as the sensibility becomes dissociated...A sense of impotence seemed frequently to overpower the poet, the heart was in an autumnal state, incapable of registering the meaning of events. 'Without meaning to perceive, what is perception' he asks?...One feels that Ghalib's ultimate theme is language, the break down of language that signifies the breakdown of relationships. His inwardness is different from Romantic subjectivity, it comes from the isolation of the poet in the city's commercial chaos; it is a desperate search for a private sense of belonging and of order created out of the cultural fragments strewn around him. He feels spiritually crippled and sterile, subjected to an entropic anarchy.[30]

Although literature like that of Ghalib's, was not a direct inspiration for modern painting it is interesting that the same sense of despair, alienation and fragmentation, that was experienced by the modern urban Indian artist, was being expressed by Ghalib through his poetry.[31]

Dissociated from literature and torn from tradition modern urban India saw the search by artists for a new human form in visual art, and this form was to emerge from the mind of the modern urban intellectual Indian artist and not the tradition, for that tradition had lost significance for modernity. The visual human form was to emerge from a mind that was robbed of its ancient fragrance and moorings, a mind that was too feeble to re-envision the cosmic *puruṣa,* a mind that was reeling from the ravages of colonisation and the shattered dreams of the post-colonial India, and a mind that was between two worlds, one dead and the other powerless to be born. In documenting the human form in visual art, and its transformation from the ancient to the modern, we are taking a glimpse into the mind that created those forms, and from that individual mind to the collective mind of the civilisation that was stressed and in a flux.

The quest for a new form perhaps signalled not only the crisis of the artist himself but of the whole cultural complex within which he worked. It is frequently said by those who defend traditionality that the concept of tradition for us in India is neither confining nor static but dynamic and flexible, and that within the ambit of tradition it permits change. Some have claimed that the Indian tradition is like a palimpsest, where the old never totally disappears but just fades and the new is over-written on it. While this may be true, the ability to permit change would certainly absolve the tradition of the charge of tyranny. However, one cannot ignore the fact that the change must stem from a certain crisis in the tradition and that the change in turn leads to tensions within the same tradition.

This fact is not stressed enough and often gets overlooked particularly by liberal thinkers who are quick to advocate change and reject the staleness of the status quo. The evolution of the human image in modern Indian art is a case in point. From the mythic art of ancient and mediaeval India where the human image was an evolution and replica of the cosmic *puruṣa* to the miniature paintings of medieval India where the human image drew its inspiration from the many Purāṇic myths and secular literature such as the *śṛṅgārarasa kavya*, the human image in ancient visual art remained within an unbroken, protected and hushed *paramparā*. The various socio-historic factors and forces in ancient and mediaeval India that were to affect the civilisation were not enough to create a significant change in the psyche of the artist or in the human form in the visual art of that period. The human image was a reflection of a certain metaphysical and religious certainty and cosmogony, and in turn that world view led to a certain human form that was both dignified, unfragmented and self-assured in our visual arts. There was this double relationship from the cosmogony to the human form and from the human form to the cosmogony: one was tied to the other, one led to the other. In other words the human form in art expressed a certain world view and the world view in turn reinforced that artistic creation of the human form.

The psychic pain created by the European civilisation which led to a rupture in the Indian artistic tradition and the unsettling events of post-colonial India led to a palpable tension within the tradition and this tension was to reflect itself in the depiction of the human form in modern Indian visual art. The story of the human form in modern Indian visual art is therefore a documentary of that pain and dislocation, alienation, fragmentation, uncertainty and deep despair felt by certain urban artists. This was not a socio-economic despair that could be vented through social protest but a despair and angst at the core of the being which questioned not only the means of gaining knowledge but more importantly the certitude of knowledge itself.

In any civilisation, art and art criticism are two independent streams of art activity, but yet one influencing the other. In ancient India we had a strong and vibrant tradition of aestheticians starting with Bharata in the first century BC right up to Paṇdit Jagannātha in the 16th century who wrote extensively on various aspects of art.. Bharata's *Nāṭyaśāstra* was so influential and venerated that it acquired the status of a quasi-scripture and was called the fifth Veda. Aesthetic experience in ancient India was given an exalted, transcendent status and aesthetic discourse always had a philosophical undertone. Vātsyāyana in writing about the *Nāṭyaśāstra* states:

> Bharata shares a world-view which is reflected in the *Upaniṣads* and is articulated in a fairly large body of literature, including the epics. Underlying the many series of categories is the concept of *avyakta* and *vykta* (unmanifest and manifest) of the one undifferentiated state of *samadhi* and concentration and the diverse expressions...He seeks to synthesize diverse disciplines and asserts that the arts have the latency

> and potency of bringing together all aspects of life, from the physical to the psychical and even metaphysical in a meaningful whole.[32]

Bharata sets the tone not only of a continuum from the secular to the sacred through the arts but places art creation within the ambits of an Idealistic Hindu world view and cosmogony.

However in the 19th century colonised India both classical art creation and art criticism not only languished but we were without a formal and sustained aesthetic discourse. There was a fragmentation between the sacred and the secular, a preference for Realism at the cost of Idealism and the birth of a narrow and rational subjectivity instead of a vast and catholic universality in matters artistic. With the birth of new artistic movements in Bengal came a number of magazines and it was in these magazines that aesthetic discourse was carried out. There were a surfeit of magazines in the late 19th and early 20th centuries which aimed to increase art awareness in their readers. There was Shilpa-Pushpanjali, Bharati, Sadhana, Pradip and Prabasi, all in Bengali and The Modern Review and Arya in English. The issues raised in these magazines make interesting reading for not only do they reflect the ethos of the urban cultivated Indian at that time, but more importantly give us a glimpse of the debate that prevailed at that time about art activity and painting in particular.

The main thrust of these magazines was to cultivate among its readers a European taste and promote a Western standard when it came to painting. European painting of the last three centuries was held up as high art and the general trend of the writing in these magazines was that modern Indian painting had not attained that level. The Kalighat paintings and those of Ravi Verma were put down as either too folkish or mythological and the work of Abanindranath was given high recognition. An analysis of the literary magazines of this period would make a good study by itself, but for our purpose it is important to note that the literati at the turn of the century were steering us away from the ancient to the modern, from the traditional to the new, from the spiritual to the rational and from Indian to Western modes of thinking about painting. In the name of Academic Realism our gods and goddesses were being dethroned and brought down to real life, our myths were being devalued and Idealistic or spiritual awareness was best jettisoned if one had to progress in this world that was increasingly being dominated by the West. That progress was equated with reason, to be elite was to be rational, to be proper was to be Western, and the order of the day was to discard the past and fashion a new and progressive Indianness in thinking and painting.

After the birth of new artistic movements in Bengal the modern Indian painter had arrived and there was no more looking back. He (or she) was an urban artist, who no longer responded to the storehouse of *Purāṇic* myths for artistic inspiration but instead reached into his mind, it was not the mind within the mind of the ancient artist which was given to *dhyāna*, but the modern mind that was totally involved emotionally with and reacted intellectually to the mundane and everyday reality of the world around him. To that cerebral mind the human condition revealed itself as much through the banality and the destitution of life, the angst and the pain of ordinary mortals, the suffering and injustice of everyday life, as through its triumphs and victories and its mythic ideals and forms. The urban intellectual let his rational faculties go unbridled, to him his very being rested on the Cartesian premise that to be was to think. It would be useful to listen to an artist and an art dealer to get a flavour of the urban artistic mind.

> Navjot: "To me, painting is not an isolated activity where one places oneself above the masses, completely untouched by hard reality, and tries to view the world in a detached manner, pumping in the metaphysical for good measure .... To me, an artist has to live within the joy and pain of the milieu. One has no right to place oneself above the greater interests of society".

> Kali Pundole on Hussain: "...he made me aware of the freedom of being unconventional, acting on the spur of the moment, not being slavish to accepted ideas of society or

> time....[38] He is sensitive, perceptive and in tune with his environment, quick to relate to situations and incidents....[33]

The modern artist found himself marching to the sounds of a tin drum and the not the beat of celestial music. For him time was profane and linear and not sacred and circular. The modern artist worked independently and often in solitude rather than in a community of artists, a solitude that not only insulated him from his fellow man but equally alienated him from the hoary past. It was in this state of solitude that he created his own private symbols and personal visual language rather than drawing upon the shared symbols and motifs of the tradition. The modern artist exhibited his work in a gallery and sought patronage in the art market rather than from the rapidly vanishing nobility and royalty. All these factors were subverting the traditional mythic mind and replacing it with rationality.

The human form in the hands of these modern urban artists was no longer idealised to express an inner reality but was an expression of reality as it is, *yathārtha.* It was an expression of *saṁsāra,* as it was experienced here and now. Beauty was not an enchanted forest where the *gopīs* danced or the majestic Kailāsa where Śiva and Pārvatī dallied. Beauty for our modern artists was seen and found equally in banality as in grandeur; the subjects of an artist's depiction were no mythic beings but the mundane and everyday human. Artistic creativity had come face to face with social realism.

Art creation in modern India, and painting in particular, has been prolific and it is difficult, if not impossible, to make any general or sweeping comments about it. Modern paintings are so individual that what can be said about the work of one artist does not apply to that of the other. A number of useful surveys have been carried out and these document the range and variety of the vast output of Indian visual artists. Unfortunately however these overviews of art cannot, and dc not, engage in a serious aesthetic discourse. Modern and contemporary art criticism in newspapers, magazines and journals, while taking note of artists and art activity, has not been able to provide a thorough and rigorous discourse. Often engaging in superficial issues such as the formal qualitites of the work of art, or clearly unaesthetic issues such as the personality or psychological make-up of the artist, or lowering it to a rupee per square inch value of a piece of art, aesthetic discourse in our time has clearly been unable to find universal or objective terms of reference of modern Indian painting. While art criticism has languished, the market place for art has brought in its own forces demands and tensions. The commerce of art favours the aggressive, the pompous, the publicity conscious artist. And equally the patronage of art can be whimsical and subjective. A high profile patron can propel a mediocre artist to fame on purely unaesthetic merits. These are the dangers of modern art activity driven by subjective norms on the part of the artist, the vagary of the market place on the other and the lack of as aesthetic discourse which could underpin art creation and criticism.

In contrast to this type of art criticism in modern India, aesthetic discourse in ancient India was more rigorous and objective. While *alaṁkāra* or adornment and *rīti* or style were used by some aestheticians as a plank in their discourse, the universal watermark of traditional aesthetic discourse was *rasa* or aesthetic emotion. The entire edifice of ancient aesthetic discourse rested on the *rasa* doctrine, a doctrine that was to hold sway for almost two millennia. The corpus of literature on *rasa* is extensive and we need not be detained by it in our quest for an understanding of the human image in modern art. However it would not be out of place if the two cardinal principles of the *rasa* doctrine are repeated and reaffirmed. First, the human condition according to the doctrine is characterised by nine or ten fundamental or basic emotions or *vibhāva*, and it is these primary or basic emotive states that can be converted into a *rasa* by the accomplished artist by an artistic bringing together of the primary emotion, secondary emotional manifestations or *anubhava* and tertiary emotional characteristics *vyabhicāribhāva*. The point to note is that the human image is of prime importance in signifying the emotion and the landscape is only secondary and subservient to the human image. Secondly, *rasa* is an *alaukika* state, a supramundane, transcendent state, not a state of superficial, hedonistic art excitement or thrill but a state of a deeply contemplative, meditative aesthetic bliss, second only to *brahmajñāna* or higher realisation. The *rasa* doctrine has played a foundational role in the whole gamut of art activity from creation to criticism in ancient India and created a centripetal force in Indian aesthetics which not only kept the various forms of art integrated but provided the main thread of continuity in our artistic tradition.

It is against this background of the foundational *rasa* doctrine that we must undertake an examination of modern visual art. Our mandate is to forge an aesthetic discourse of modern art and not engage in mere art chatter. If we are to call ourselves aesthetes of modern art we must discourse about that art within the parameters of the *rasa* doctrine, a doctrine that is not only uniquely Indian but one that has stood the test of time. By doing so we not only ensure a continuity between the past and the present but equally raise and deepen the level of art criticism of modern art. Limiting our inquiry into the depiction of the human image in modern Indian painting, the question that then arises is whether or not our modern artists use the nine or ten conventional rasas, or is there a new *rasa* afoot, a *rasa* that was not recognised by Bharata and not displayed in traditional art and one that our modern urban artists have needed to express the human condition as they experienced it. If a new *rasa* is indeed found in modern painting, a *rasa* that did not appear in traditional and ancient art, then it would not be wrong to make the claim that this *rasa* is unique to the condition of modernity for us in India, and that further we can assert that this *rasa* actually defines modernity for us. A further question would then be how and why this *rasa* was not a part of the ancient artistic tradition.

For one who is steeped in ancient visual art the most arresting feature of modern Indian painting, that sets it apart from traditional visual art, is the fragmentation and distortion of the human image in the creations of some of our urban artists. By no means a universal phenomenon, this fragmentation and truncation is so arresting, and obviously untraditional, that it captures our attention and demands that we do not bypass it as something trivial, but take careful note of it, and establish a discourse around it. Such a discourse would not only throw light on the modern human form but importantly on modernity itself. As Vātsyāyana correctly observes "lines ... are symbolic of inner states of mind"[34] and fragmented lines must indeed reflect an inner state of fragmentation and distortion.

Instead of the proudly erect, majestically graceful, equipoised in every limb and gesture, defying the limitations of time and space, the *puruṣa* of ancient art has been transformed, by some of our modern artists, into a fragmented, tortuous, truncated, debilitated man. Unable to stand proud and tall, modern man becomes a victim of his own mind. Defeated by the weight of the world around him and burdened by his own mind he can neither stand tall and erect like Surya, nor sit equipoised like Gaṇeśa, nor rest in perfect stillness like the *śeṣaśāyī* Viṣṇu, nor assume the posture of serenity of the Buddha, nor dance majestically like the Naṭarāja, nor maintain the sensuous *tribhaṅga* pose of Pārvatī or stride lightly on a *haṁsa* like Sarasvatī. The image of the cosmic *puruṣa* is held in dynamic harmony through the centripetal energy exuding from the navel. The movements and deflections of the body, or *bhangās*, of the cosmic *puruṣa* are circular and gentle, a movement that ends in the still centre of energy or the *bindu.* The *bindu* is also the *bīja,* the seed from which everything grows and to which it returns through a system of multilayered correspondences.

The composition whether on the stage as in drama, or plastic as in sculpture, was a micro-representation of the universe, and was charged with a certain energy and rhythm, and represented the Hindu world view. The movements of the modern fragmented man in painting on the other hand are frenzied and erratic and lack grace or coherence, without a *bindu* or a *bīja* to hold these movements together. Grim faced and with eyes sullen and bereft of radiance, the modern man of the modern artist seems crushed by the depravity of the world around him. His hands are devoid of the beautiful *mudrās* of the Purāṇic beings but are instead writhing in agony. His tottering feet are unable to dance to the beat of time, while some others are often devoid of feet or have amputated feet. The ethos of the anthropomorphic form of the cosmic *puruṣa* is transpersonal and transcendent, for even though he manifests in a human form, he is not contained by it, he defies time and space, the mundane and the particular. The modern man on the other hand is limited and confined by the structure of the human form and is unable even to maintain its grace, dignity and integrity and incapable of suggesting transcendence. Many are the symbols and motifs of transcendence of traditional art, whether it be the uplifted left leg of the Nataraja, or the lotus pedestal, or the *karaṇās* and *bhangās* of the body, or the thirty-two *lakṣaṇas* of a *mahāpuruṣa* on the body of the Buddha, cosmic signs such as the crescent moon on the head of Śiva, the raised finger of Kṛiṣṇa as he lifts mount Govardhana and the myriad other artistic attributes of the anthropomorphic form of the cosmic *puruṣa.* Equally, the seed or the *bīja* of the composition which assures centripetality confers to it the stillness and serenity of transcendence.

The question then for the modern aesthetician is to arrive at a proper cognizance of this fragmented human image set in a banal landscape. In coming to an understanding of the complex, varied and changing human image in modern Indian art it not enough just to document the superficial structural features of that image, although a structural analysis is obviously important and is the first step. It would be easy to get entangled in the superficial and formal particulars of the image, as modern artists are so individualistic not only in their themes but in the choice of their motifs and symbols; to do so would be to miss the forest for the trees. Neither are we interested in establishing any hierarchy or a taxonomy of these fragmented human images. Our endeavour is to seek universal truths from particular observations, to move away from the surface to the depths of the mind of the modern urban artist, from a superficial art encounter to a meaningful and chastening art experience, for only then could we attempt to come to an understanding of modernity for us in India. This is the task of the modern Indian aesthetician. He is not interested in an arid discourse nor trivial art chatter, but in probing the human condition as revealed in modern Indian paintings.

Traditional Indian aesthetics had a long and close link with religion on the one hand and with philosophy on the other. The terms of philosophic discourse were already in place and Indian aesthetics right from the start took an Idealist stance. It is but appropriate that the *Nāṭyaśāstra* was called the fifth Veda. Coomaraswamy was wrong when he said that art is the hand maid of religion and equally wrong were they who gave aesthetic experience a metaphysical status. But what is correct to say is that aestheticians while pursuing an independent stream of thought were never very far from the other two streams. Philosophical Idealism and sectarian theology were kindred doctrines to these traditional aestheticians. Abhinavagupta while writing extensively and probingly on the *rasa* doctrine was also the high priest of Kāshmīr Śaivism. The eight traditional *rasas* and later the ninth and the tenth were understood and celebrated in an ambience of cultural stability and epistemic certainty. Despite conquests and invasions the joyous and optimistic Hindu spirit that promised ultimate knowledge and realisation to everyone remained untouched.

The *karma* doctrine through the millennia remained unchallenged, and right through the various dynasties and empires, kings and nobility and other patrons of art there was never a sense of godlessness or existentialism that was publicly proclaimed in thought or art. This is not to deny individual or transient or private states of existentialism. These must have existed, as doubt and uncertainty are as much a part of the human condition as are hope and faith. But existentialism as a philosophy was never enunciated in ancient or mediaeval India. The *karma* doctrine in all its shades of meaning was never seriously or systematically questioned, death was never considered final, and time never understood as linear but circular. So pervasive was the influence of the *karma* doctrine that even Indian Muslims and Christians, for whom *karma* is not doctrinally justified, speak of a previous life and a future birth. Urban intellectuals of modern India, and some artists in particular, adopting a frame of discourse have reacted to the unprecedented socio-economic disparity of modern

India, to the unmitigated sense of hopelessness of the urban poor, the social injustice of the downtrodden, the widespread decay in moral and ethical values in society and the alienation of society from its roots and moorings. Surely they argued what collective *karma* could account for this state of affairs. Which God would dispense such a punishment? Is there an explanation for this state of uncertainty and hopelessness and chaos in the world around them?

Fired by these and other existentialist feelings an urban intellectual who feels a sense of angst, alienation and existential despair would react in different ways. Some might vent their feelings in creative writing, others in pursuing a path of social and political activism and protest, while the artistically inclined would express themselves in their visual creations. It is important to note that the painter or the writer in expressing this sense of existential despair is not reacting to his or her own personal situation in life, but rather at society, or segments of it, around him. This despair must be distinguished from a state of depression or discontent that an individual may experience, for depression is a primarily a psychological state while despair is both an epistemic and ontologic state. The existential despair of modern artists is neither an autobiographical nor a personal lament, but an experience of a more universal hopelessness and stark bleakness at the state of the human condition. In the absence of a systematic existential philosophy it was left to our artists to express this emotion through the fragmented human body and the banality of the landscape around it.

We would like to make the claim that this fragmented human image that we have been speaking of in modern Indian art, stems from the emotion of existential despair which is a new emotion in the Indian tradition and seems to be the emotion that defines modernity in India. The human image in art, which takes its pedigree from the cosmic *puruṣa* of the *puruṣa sūkta* of the Ṛg Veda, was able to express the ten basic emotions of the tradition through anthropomorphic terms without there being any fragmentation or distortion. Through *hastas* and *bhangas*, through *abhinaya* and *alaṁkāra*, the human image whether it was in *nāṭya* or *śilpa, kāyva* or *citra,* was a repository of those ten emotions. Existential despair which questions the very premise of *mokṣa* or spiritual freedom through ultimate and perfect knowledge, must indeed splinter the image of the impregnable *puruṣa* into that of a fragmented man. When the certitude of ultimate knowledge itself is being questioned, and uncertainty marks the human psyche, the visual paradigm of that perfect knowledge, the integral image of the *puruṣa,* a *puruṣa* with a thousand heads, must crumble into a thousand pieces. And equally the landscape of that fragmented man in modern art bears no resemblance to the ordered space surrounding the cosmic *puruṣa.*

If one accepts that the fragmented human image in modern Indian art is a sign of existential despair then the next task is to situate this emotion within the framework of the *rasa* doctrine. If *nastik nairaiśya* or existential despair is the basic *sthayibhava, mānava rasa* is the *rasa* of that *nairaśya.* It is the *rasa* of the modern urban intellectual, a *rasa* born of unbridled rationality, that puts man in the centre of the universe, of a state of being that finds that this is a godless world devoid of cosmic justice, of a sense of helplessness and a bleak realisation that we are mere mortals in a chaotic world, of a feeling of absurdity of this historical time-bound existence, of a lack of certainty of ultimate knowledge. A noted Canadian intellectual put it succinctly when she said, "This world as clearly seen is seen through tears, why then do you ask what is wrong with my eyes?"[35]

This *mānava rasa* would be then be the *rasa* that defines modernity for us in India. Giving this emotion the status of a *rasa* ensures that we are able to include some, if not all, of our modern art within the *parampara* of the *rasa* doctrine, rather than letting it drift away from the main stream of aesthetics. The *rasa* doctrine has grown dynamically from the eight rasas of Bharata to the ninth or *Śānta rasa* of Abhinavagupta and the tenth or *bhakti rasa* of mediaeval India, a *rasa* that was created by bifurcating *śṛṅgāra rasa* into the sacred and the secular. Both the ninth and tenth *rasas* were by-products of socio-historic changes in our civilisation, and the *rasas* in turn moulded our aesthetic sensibilities. *Śānta rasa* was largely the result of the influence of

Buddhist thought and the emergence of the bhakti *rasa* was the outcome of the rising presence of Islam in our country. Both *śānti* and *bhakti rasas* were expressed by our artists, be they *kavis* or *śilpīs*, and in turn the artistic expression influenced and nurtured the psyche of the Indian civilisation. It is but appropriate that modernity for us in India, which has seen a significant break from the past in many different and significant ways, usher in a new *rasa*. The *rasa* doctrine is not only the foundational aesthetic doctrine for us in India but equally it has been responsible for maintaining a thread of continuity, not only in aesthetic criticism, but in binding the different art forms into an integral whole. It is *rasa* that moved us away from the superficial aspects of art such as *rīti* and *alaṁkāra* into a deeper, more catholic and a chastened contemplative art realisation and experience.

While the traditional aesthetician was able to tap into the established terms of philosophical discourse, the modern aesthetician on the other hand has to strike out on his own as he treads virgin territory, particularly as new images demand new concepts, and there is no definitive philosophy that can be called modern and yet Indian. The rich and profound philosophical tradition in India came to an end with the *bhakti* movement and *viśiṣṭādvaita* was the last chapter in the book of Indian philosophy. Nineteenth century Indian philosophers like Shri Ramakrishna and his illustrious disciple Vivekananda, Ramanna Maharshi and Sri Aurobindo did not postulate any basically new philosophical doctrines but merely reinterpreted well established ideas. Although we are aware of the contrary view, we take the stand that socio-historic conditions of the day do have a major impact on ideas and ideologies, philosophy and religion. In this sense neither philosophy nor religion, and therefore the arts, can be divorced from social realities and the world around it.

Ours is a not a monolithic or closed tradition. New ideas, new emotions, new images, new *rāgas*, new forms are being formed and if they are significant, and if society which includes connoisseurs and consumers, accept these new evolutions, then these new developments are incorporated in the growing and evolving tradition. While we cannot make a claim that existentialism is by any means the dominant thought of modern India, we feel confident, on the basis of the fragmented human image, that it has been expressed often enough by some urban artists, and that this in many ways defines modernity in India. *Mānava rasa*, while not claiming to be a philosophical doctrine, is indeed an expression of a state of being of modernity. Some may argue that *guru* toting religiosity and right wing, politically inspired, Hindu fundamentalism, is a feature of twentieth century India, and that this denies and refutes existentialism; that the thrust of the times is towards a quest for God rather than away from it. Our response to that argument would be that this form of God seeking is a reaction to, rather than an expression of existentialism, and would probably constitute part of the syndrome of post-modernism for us in India.

We have repeatedly stressed that the feeling of despair is an urban phenomenon, felt by urban intellectuals, created in urban spaces and exhibited in urban art galleries. Rural artists do not seem to have experienced despair of this sort, and even if they have, they would portray it through their ritual art, and not through the fragmented human image. Rural India has been saved largely, though not totally, from the ravages of modernity. Where people are close to the soil, where terracota is one of the main materials of artistic expression, where motifs of adornment express not only their harmony with nature but equally the magic of growth and the promise of fertility, where there is no hierarchy between art and craft, and where arid rationality has not erased treasured memories of millennia of myth, existential despair is not likely to set in. It is clear that there is something about the modern Indian urban environment that is responsible for the fostering, experience and expression of despair. The rational mind, or *buddhi*, moves in linear rather than circular time, affirms reality that is immediate and questions the ultimate, does not confront dialectic but prefers to assert one or the other, insists that things are either black or white but not grey, excels in the fragmentation of thought, and delights in creating dualities.

Recognising existential despair as a *rasa* of modernity is not only important but urgent. Its time has come. In matters artistic, as in philosophy, it is more important to raise the right questions in seeking the right answers. The central question for the modern aesthetician then is, what is the deeper meaning of the fragmented human image? Should it be dismissed as an outpouring of a disturbed mind, an artistic aberration, whimsical creativity or the doodling of a discontented state of being? Surely not. The colonial experience is too fresh in our minds to forget how our colonisers misunderstood, misrepresented and distorted many aspects of our traditional culture and civilisation. If we are to avoid a repetition of the agenda of Orientalism it is important that we take stock of the fragmented human image in our prolific modern visual art, initiate the right aesthetic discourse around it and leave it in caring hands, hands that will ensure that the art is not only catalogued and archived, and exposed to the market place of art, but more importantly deeply understood, meaningfully enjoyed and properly celebrated. Not to do so would be doing an injustice to modern Indian creativity. The time honoured *rasa* doctrine served our ancient and mediaeval art, and *mānava rasa* can do the same for the fragmented human image of our modern art. In traditional Indian aesthetics, the stream of aesthetic discourse flowed parallel to the streams of philosophical speculation and religious doctrine. *Mānava rasa* could initiate an existentialist discourse for us in India, for a *rasa* is incomplete without it being underpinned by a philosophical system. Equally a *rasa,* though free standing, could have ethical and axiological considerations as an outcome.

It has rightly been said that all ideas in the web of knowledge are inter-connected and aesthetics though free standing and autonomous cannot exist in a void. While the first eight *rasas* are underpinned by the *agamas* in general and Kāshmīr Śaivism in particular, the ninth *rasa* of peace is supported by Buddhist doctrines and the tenth *rasa* of *bhakti* by *viśiṣṭādvaita.* Since we have visual evidence of an existential state of being in modern India in the form of the fragmented human image we must take a bold step in enunciating an existentialist philosophy to provide the foundation for *mānava rasa,* and further explore if this modern *rasa* can be linked to any socio-political ideas on the other. Perhaps the modern Indian brand of existentialism may be different from such philosophies that have been developed in the West, and it would be in the fitness of things that we in India, exposit our own existential philosophy, from within the tradition, rather than letting an outsider do it for us. This would not only recognise the primacy of our artists who were not only brave but strident in choosing the fragmented human image in giving vent to a feeling, but it would equally enhance the fearless Indian tradition which had the strength and the vision to proclaim in the hoary past *aham brahmāsmi.*

While a *rasa* is enjoyed and celebrated on its own merit and for its own sake, and while the doctrine is self-standing, autonomous and non-sectarian, it supports a certain ambience and world view. It is interesting to note that while rural and folk art are an important part of the Indian artistic repository, it was the urban elite who was considered the aesthete par excellence. A portrait of such an aesthete emerges in many ancient writings but none so vivid as in Vātsyāyana's Kamasutra. It was this cultivated urban elite, the *nagārika,* with an aesthetic flare and finesse who enjoyed and promoted the arts. *Bhakti rasa* of mediaeval India brought in its unique ethos of temple centred art activities and went hand in hand with the entire *bhakti* cult with its gamut of social and ethical manifestations. The urban *nagarika* and the *bhakta* are too well known to need further elaboration. It would be an appropriate question to ask, what then would be ethical manifestations of *mānava rasa,* who would be its prototypical aesthete?

The recognition of existential despair, its artistic expression by modern urban intellectuals in the form of the fragmented human image and its celebration by the modern and contemporary aesthete could possibly lead to *mānavtā* or humanness. The *mānavtā* of modern India would be similar to the Buddhist concept of *karuna* or compassion and care for the entire world and would also echo the ancient Hindu sentiment of *vasudhaiva kuṭumbakam* but with one major difference. Modern *mānavtā* would stem from the realisation that although this is a godless world, a world devoid of cosmic justice, a world where there is neither *karma* nor *īśvara*, that it is a world of stark hopelessness and downright absurdity, not just for the individual but for many others around him, and that he is not alone in that predicament. The realisation that this state of despair is not unique but widespread, if not universal, releases the individual and gives him a sense of relief and freedom. In that state of release he comes to the realiṣation that it behoves him to care and serve his fellow man for he too is in a similar world. It is not difficult to see that shades of the ethics of *mānavtā* could have been the spring of the political ideology of socialism and the welfare state, ideologies which are the contributions of political science to modernity.

ENDNOTES

1. Ranjit Hoskote. Intuitive Logic, The Next Step. Heart. 1999. p. 21.
2. Carl Jung. Man and His Symbols. New York. Double Day & Company. Inc. 1964. p. 250.
3. Lloyd and Susanne Rudolph. The Modernity of Tradition. Chicago. The University of Chicago Press. 1967. pp 3-4.
4. Shanti Swarup. The Times of India. February 28, 1998.
5. K. Satchidanandan. Literature: Signing in Different Scripts, in Independent India, The First Fifty Years. Delhi. Indian Council for Cultural Relations. Oxford University Press. 1998. p. 353.
6. Andre Beattie. The Times of India. December 14, 1998.
7. K. Satchidananda, Literature: Signing in Different Scripts in Independent India The First Fifty Years. Delhi. Indian Council for Cultural Relations. Oxford University Press. 1998. p. 356.
8. *yastva vijnānavānbhavatyayuktena manasā sadā, tasyendriyanyavasyāni dustāśvāiva saratheh.* Kaṭhopaniṣad. 3.5
9. *etavanasya mahimā, eto jyāyāṁśca purusah. Puruṣa Sūkta.* 1.3
10. *na tasya pratimā asti yasya nāma mahadyaśaḥ.* Śvetāśvatara Upaniṣad.
11. Original by Dadu translated by Rabindranath Tagore, quoted in N. Ray. Idea and Image in Indian Art. Delhi. Munshiram Manoharlal Publishers. 1973. p. 5
12. Chāndogya Upaniṣad. 6.12

13. Mulk Raj Anand, The Hindu View of Art. Bombay. Asia Publishing House, 1957. pp. 75-76.
14. Nirmal Verma. India and Europe: The Self and the Other. India International Centre Quarterly. Volume 20, 1993. p. 138.
15. ibid. p. 141.
16. ibid. p. 141.
17. ibid. p. 142.
18. ibid. p. 147.
19. Kṛiṣṇa Iyer. Making a Difference. A Collection of Essays (ed.) Rukmini Sekhar. Spic Macay. 1998. p 6.
20. Satyapal Anand. Indian Perspectives. Delhi. Ministry of External Affairs. November 1991. p. 40.
21. Tapati Guha-Thakurta. The Making of a New Indian Art. Cambridge University Press. 1992. p. 16.
22. ibid. p. 18.
23. ibid. p. 19.
24. ibid. p. 110.
25. ibid. p. 111.
26. K. Satchidananda. p. 357.
27. Tapati Guha-Thakurta. p. 82.
28. Kapila Vātsyāyana. Personal communication.
29. Devangana Desai. The Times of India. December 9, 1997.
30. K. Satchidananda. p. 354.
31. I am grateful to Ashok Vajpayee for encouraging me to look into the poetry of Ghalib to understand the roots of modernity in India.
32. Kapila Vātsyāyana. Bharata, The *Nāṭyaśāstra.* Delhi. Sahitya Akademi. 1996. p. 21.
33. The Times of India. December 10, 1997.
34. Kapila Vatsysyan. The Square and the Circle of Indian Art. Delhi. Roli Books International. 1983. p. 110.
35. Margaret Atwood is a noted Canadian intellectual. This statement is attributed to her.

5

Ancient Homes to Modern Homelessness

Ranjit Hoskote

I. Introduction: The Condition of Spiritual Homelessness

No greater fallacy has afflicted the realm of the arts than the fallacy by which tradition is conceived of as a timeless and immutable entity, a construct immune to the vagaries of history. Essentialist as it is, such a conception of tradition lays great store by the value of continuity which becomes, in this account, an automatic guarantee of location, identity and purpose to the individuals assembled within the normative space of the tradition. Tradition, in other words, serves the individual as a home.

Consider, therefore, the psychological import of this reading of tradition, as it impinges upon the endeavours of those individuals so gifted with the expressive faculties that society renders them the ambivalent honour of describing them as 'artists'. So impressive and mythic a view of tradition can have the opposite effect than the one intended on its inheritors: equally afraid of appearing derivative or betraying their ancestors, they often reel under the burden of a past that Marx once evocatively described as weighing "like a nightmare on the brain of the living".

Naturally, the most vital traditions, or the living traditions, never answer to this constricting and oppressive model. This is because they are not reliquaries of past glory so much as they are special forms of modernity, which make manifest and available to the present the resources of the generations that have gone before. Such traditions are, to use an image that I find particularly compelling, renewable resources rather than fossil fuels; to regard tradition as a static mould of perfection is to ransom the living to the dead. Necrolatry of that order only leads to distortions and misjudgements like the belief that every contemporary crisis has been experienced before in the same form, so that the resolutions of the past may be applied in the present without much need for adaptation.

This belief can leads us into a false universalism, in the grip of which we may be tempted to collapse the differences between historical periods and cultures in such a sweeping fashion as, for instance, to translate Bhartṛhari's anguish as Camus in Sanskrit costume or Wittgenstein's relentless self-questioning as an updated version of Hīnayāna discipline, postmarked Mitteleuropa. Differences evaporate before the measure of such a grand account, leaving behind the most superficial similarities, which do not help us at all in an analytical enterprise; sometimes, it is the differences that point the way to the true affinities, like those which connect post-colonial Indian painters like Raza and Gobhai to an Euro-American art tradition in which Kandinsky and Rothko play a crucial role.

The moral of the cautionary tale is that, when scholars are persuaded to replace inward criteria with outward categories as standards of comparison, the project of historical comparison is reduced to a mockery. Outward categories are defined on the basis of formal notions like genre, theme and mood; inward criteria, on the other hand, are defined by an examination of texts in relation to their contexts. The former definition is the result of a fossil manoeuvre; the latter springs from a renewability perspective.

When tradition is conceived of under the aspect of renewability, therefore, we find ourselves able to formulate a far more tenable comparison between ancient artists and their modern descendants. A comparison of this nature would permit us to note the similarity of their moral and aesthetic crises, without negating the pertinent differences that distinguish them apart as, in fact, ancient and modern artists.

In the course of this essay, I hope to attend to the condition that I will here designate as spiritual homelessness. While arguing, as a general principle, that this condition has afflicted the artist in all periods, I will attempt to demonstrate the very different nuances and emphases that spiritual homelessness acquires; these nuances and emphases depend upon the wider cultural paradigm in whose terms the artist in question has conducted his life and practice.

These thoughts are sought to be placed against the historical experience of the Indian subcontinent: contrary to the belief that Indian communities are long-rooted social clusters, it is more truly the case that migration and displacement, diaspora and resettlement have been recurrent features of traditional Indian life, especially in the north-western frontier regions. Spiritual homelessness becomes a corollary to this state of ceaseless discontinuity; accordingly, exile, migration, loss, and the loss of the self's location become recurrent themes in the arts. In religious thought, too, the question of how to achieve the state of being at home or being in one's right mind takes primacy as, for instance, in the Chāndogya Upaniṣad and the Īśa Upaniṣad.

In tracing a brief, and therefore necessarily abstract and highly idiosyncratic, history of spiritual homelessness in Indian culture, I will take the poet-dramatist Kālidāsa as my point of departure, following the trail back to the Upaniṣads and forward to post-colonial Indian art. The continuity of theme, attitude and concern over a millennium is, of course, an illusory continuity. For it is graphed across several historical ruptures, not the least of which is the advent of the rationalist position that assumed the status of the dominant intellectual paradigm during the colonial period.

This variety of rationalism constructed itself, for reasons arising out of the specific political and cultural history of post-Renaissance Europe, in a deliberately anti-metaphysical armature. Originally phrased as a challenge to the totalitarian claims advanced by the Church over every department of existence, rationalism came to reject entirely the claims of sacred culture on everyday life. This became the first move towards the establishment of an enlightened and progressive society, in which reason, rather than faith, governed human affairs.

This rejection of the sacred, as an abiding source of certitude and value, has a very specific bearing on the role and self-image of the artist. It can rob him of the confidence to operate in a familiar universe, or alternatively, it might emancipate him into an awareness of his skills of negotiation in an unfamiliar one; and if it can deepen his understanding of his own space and time, it could also grant him the ability to act independently of these parameters. Since the principle of *dharma* has long served as a mode of negotiating among the ethical, the aesthetic and the sacred in the Indian context, it assumes a critical importance in our discussion.

It is vital to bear in mind the changing importance of *dharma* in relation to the aesthetic life. The artist of Kālidāsa's time (considering the controversy over Kālidāsa's exact dates, it is to an intellectual rather than a chronological period that we refer) had a specific understanding of *dharma*, against which his actions were foregrounded; the artist who accepts the Upaniṣadic account has a particular conception of *dharma* too; but the contemporary artist is on his own in this sense, for he lives in the time after the trans-valuation of all values has taken place, and his moral responsibility is defined in terms of individual conscience rather than collective law. In all three situations, however, the crucial question for the artist is that of location and of the definition of the self in relation to the world. In other words, the central preoccupation of the artist, and in this, he dramatises the central if unarticulated concern of all sentient beings, is finding his place.

We will, therefore, first examine an artist at work in a sacred framework of action that breaks down at a boundary condition, so generating the possibility of a self-understanding which can illuminate the apparent constraints of identity, space and time (Kālidāsa). Second, we will examine a sacred framework of action that promises transcendence by emancipating the self from the particulars of identity, space and time (the Upaniṣads). The implications of the first position will be considered under the rubric of a project of somewhereness; the implications of the second will be placed under the rubric of a project of nowhereness.

Finally, we will examine the psychological and aesthetic repercussions attendant upon the loss of such sacred frameworks of action, as in the case of post-colonial Indian art, and the extent to which the two alternative projects proposed by the tradition can provide inspiration to artists in contemporary India.

II. The Yakśa's Despair: Exile and Redemption in Kālidāsa's Meghadūtam

I reserve the right to operate from an utterly old-fashioned understanding of the artist's vocation, even in an epoch during which very many artists have turned their backs on the aesthetic establishment with its baggage of canons, criteria, values and so forth, and swung around to a deliberately anti-aesthetic position. I will choose, for the purposes of this essay, to regard the artist as an individual who has dedicated himself to those moments of heightened awareness and expressivity, of responsiveness and creativity, through which our knowledge of ourselves and the world is ineffably altered. In other words, I see the artist as a questor after the sublime; his quest is no easy one, and is plagued by the shadows of disquiet. If the artist survives at all in a firm awareness of this quest, it is because the rough passage is illumined and guided by a vision of transcendence.

If we were to encapsulate this quest in an allegory, we could see the artist taking on the aspect of the lover, the part; the object with which he seeks union is the beloved, the whole. As Plato phrases the sentiment through one of the characters in the dialogue, Symposium: "Love is nothing but the name given to the desire and pursuit of the whole." In Kālidāsa's Meghadūtam, which forms the key text in this section of the essay, we find the relationship between Self and Other, the part and the whole, elaborated through an interplay of distance and communion, belonging and exile.

As the Yakṣa, the protagonist of the poem, confesses in the opening verses, he has brought his banishment upon himself by failing in his duty to his master, Kubera; this dereliction of duty is the direct result of his enraptured contemplation of his wife. Love and duty are the two poles of the Yakśa's psychological world: an excess of the former leads to indulgence and the dereliction of duty; an excess of the latter leads to alienation and the neglect of the loved one. The entire conflict is mapped across the distance between the place of belonging and the place of exile, which also embody two opposed models of time and being.

The action of Meghadūtam is determined by the tension between these two models. Alakāpurī, the protagonist's home, is the site of mythic time where it is eternally spring and the affliction of change is unknown; Rāmagiri, where he has been exiled, is the site of real time, bound by the cycle of the seasons and the vicissitudes of change. The Yakśa's despair is caused by the fact that he has been exiled, banished, cast out, made separate from the reality he was accustomed to regard as his own. This displacement, with the discontinuity and alienation that it entails, is the sign of the Yakśa's fall from the state of eternity into the condition of time.

In the frame of mythic time, action is governed by the ceremonial rules of conduct; any contravention of these invites instant penalty. The only permissible mode of securing redemption in mythic time, therefore, is the ability to adhere to protocol, the paradigm by which the part maintains its relationship with the whole. In the frame of real time, however, it is individual action, which is determined by a combination of energy and wisdom, a mooring in propriety tempered by an alertness to opportunity, that is more crucial than programmatic rules of conduct. By this reasoning, it becomes obvious that strategy is the only plausible mode of securing redemption in real time; strategy, here, designates the variety of means by which the part, when separated from the whole, addresses its desire to what it has lost.

When the part is cut adrift from the whole or, in Kālidāsa's terms, the lover separated from the beloved, it has recourse to memory: to invoke what it has lost, to re-fashion the world which it once knew intimately. Memory, after all, is the sign that you no longer belong to the remembered space; memory is the sign of being other than and apart from what is remembered. In this process of remembering, which is remembering the unconscious and even blissful state of belonging becomes transformed into a conscious and even restless condition of cathexis: the naive becomes the sentimental, in Schiller's terms, and art is born.

As Chandra Rajan observes, in the Introduction to her translation of a selection of Kālidāsa's writings, 1 Kālidāsa's vision centres on the recurrent curse-exile-penance leitmotif as a pattern of the self's evolution through tribulation to perfection. The fuller cycle of psychological and real events in the Meghadūtam narrative may be described under the curse-fall-penance-restoration leitmotif; but the point to be made here is that the narrative evolves from the conflict between love and duty. In this conflict, which is the dialectic of passion and reflection in disguise, the curse is a necessary brake or pause that permits the narrative to become a mode of self-awareness, and therefore healing and redemption. In another variant of this reading, the art-work can be conceived of as being, always, the Self's apostrophe, an address to the Other, who is always absent, invisible, unapproachable, fleeing. This pursuit may lead to an ambivalence of attitude: there are, for instance, competing elements of nostalgia, melodrama, quietism and stoicism in the Yakṣa's eloquent apology.

The point at issue here is that Kālidāsa does not divorce the conceptual realm of ethical crisis from the experiential realm of sensuous stimuli, but maps the one onto the other in such a way that we can only approach the ethical project by means of our involvement in an aesthetic exploration. It is not by separating the detached *sākṣī*, or witnessing consciousness, from the impassioned *rasika* or enjoying consciousness in our reading of the text, but by accepting the responsibility of *rasika*-hood as a precondition to *sākṣī*-hood that we will make any progress in this drama.

My argument here is that Kālidāsa embeds the dialectic between love and duty so deeply into an aesthetic conception of the world that the values he communicates, so far from springing from an external system of ethics, are produced by the unfolding of the text itself. The aesthetic encounter becomes, therefore, a source of existential values or *dharma*, by releasing the self from the stylised and circumscribed space of mythic time into the chaos of real time, it instigates the crucial passage of the self from protocol to strategy. So transformed, the self becomes the bearer of a dynamic praxis, whilst before, it had been the bearer of a static nomos.

In concluding this brief consideration of Kālidāsa's poem, we may remark that *rasabodha,* wisdom attained through aesthetic encounter, has been conceived of here as an independent mode of *mokṣa,* the understanding of the world, so as to overcome it. Indeed, it is shown to be as valid and important a mode of *mokṣa* as *jñānabodha,* which is wisdom attained through the cultivation of knowledge.

III. The World as Home: The Upaniṣadic Account

The image of the *sākṣī* and the *rasika* as two aspects of the self is one that the Upaniṣads enshrine in the perennial image of the two birds who share a branch: one eats a fruit, while the other watches it eat. This image emphasises the dynamic and dialogic nature of the relationship, for the Upaniṣads do not so much offer a table of answers as they do a style of inquiry.

The central question of the Upaniṣads is this: How do we understand the self in its relation to the world, the spirit in its relation to the body, and where, finally, are we at home? In other words: How does one establish a mode of belonging? This question takes on a considerable urgency when we consider the history of migration, both voluntary and forced, that has defined the identity of many individuals and communities through human history; and certainly, as we have noted in passing, Indian history.

One way to establish a mode of belonging is that commonly practised by communities, nations and states, which we may designate as the project of somewhereness. In this perspective, place is regarded as insurance; space is invested with emotional and mythic associations. From this arise the many *sthala purāṇas* or place legends; at their best, these are versions rather than claims, but they may degenerate into territorial ideologies. The project of somewhereness is often a collective cultural project, and its communitarian expression in traditional literature is the *itihāsa*; and yet, the thought occurs to us that the project of somewhereness can also assume a highly individualistic expression, as it does in so accomplished and richly imagined a *kāvya* as Meghadūtam.

Another and radically different way to establish a mode of belonging is that proposed by the Upaniṣads: the re-creation of a plan, more spiritual than spatial, to replace the lost homeland. We might usefully think of this as the project of nowhereness, which considers the world as home. To this line of thinking, the transformation of the self and the refinement of its consciousness is the most effective means of renewing the world. An individual project, it anchors itself in an eternal present in which the specificities of space and time are treated merely as incidental details relevant to transient personalities, but not to the self that takes on these roles from life to life; in the eternal present, these details have been planed away, all conflicts and their residues have been distilled away, and the self stands in no need of enacting the drama of life to attain an understanding of its deepest motives and its identity.

This is the conception of *mokṣa*; and here, we may derive a model from the persuasive Upaniṣadic metaphor of the city of *brahman*, celebrated in the Chāndogya Upaniṣad. In that text we find a beautiful trope of world-renewal in the line: "As great as the infinite space beyond is the space within the lotus of the heart."[2] The Upaniṣadic lotus of the heart enshrines the key concept of *dharma*: in this context; it acquires a spiritual charge, signifies the heroic overcoming of the self and its circumstances by the cultivation of perfect thought and conduct, perfect self-knowing, the transcendence of the particular markers and boundaries of personal identity.

Where the project of somewhereness emphasises discontinuity and locality, the project of nowhereness emphasises pattern and cosmology; and while the project of somewhereness depends on an apocalyptic narrative of collapse from the scale of eternity into the scale of chronology, the project of nowhereness elides such opposed conceptions of time altogether, permitting the individual subject to be at home in all contexts and situations. While the *rasika*, the bird of somewhereness tastes the fruit of experience, reacting to its changing shape and flavour in various ways, the *sākṣī*, the bird of nowhereness, preserves its detachment from the fruit of experience without losing its sensitivity and compassion.

This essay will argue that, far from remaining confined to the realm of the antiquarian student of texts, these two approaches to the fundamental questions of human existence exert a considerable influence on the manner in which we may view the endeavours and achievements of many contemporary artists. The dialogue between the two perspectives is not only enacted at the level of thought and discussion, but is given concrete embodiment in the art-work itself; like Kālidāsa's Yakṣa, the contemporary artist in India strives towards a *rasabodha*, not escaping from life into aesthetic encounter, but treating aesthetic encounter as the stage where the deepest questions of being may be enacted.

IV. Homeless in the Present: The Alternatives before Indian Art

This is the moment, perhaps, at which to address ourselves to the manner in which post-colonial Indian artists have drawn upon these two models, or modes by which a spiritual homeland is re-created to replace a lost geographical or psychological homeland-which we have outlined in the course of this essay. The first, the project of somewhereness, associated here with Kālidāsa, takes the form of the creation, as it were, of a new world of objects, an environment re-constituted through art. The second, the project of nowhereness, associated here with the Upaniṣads, takes the form of a meditation on the numinous and the transcendental aspect of the universe, to the exclusion or dilution of its more local and immediate attributes.

This essay will now examine the appeal that these modes have held for post-colonial Indian artists, including painters like S H Raza, Jehangir Sabavala, Akbar Padamsee, J Swaminathan, Laxman Shreshtha and Mehlli Gobhai, who pursue the modernist tradition of the Kandinsky circle in Europe and the much later Rothko circle in America, yet modulate these inheritances by reference to their concern with Indian metaphysical accounts. Through their work, it may be possible to study the contemporary outcomes that emerge when the artistic desire enters into a space of encounter with the phenomenal world from which the human consciousness has been expelled.

Sharing as they do in the condition of spiritual homelessness, or homelessness in the present, Raza, Sabavala, Padamsee, Swaminathan, Shreshtha, Gobhai and many of their contemporaries are artists who indicate the possibility of transcendence through a perception of the sublime that is mediated concretely through the art-work. The question that has possessed all these artists is: How to invest the world of objects with the aura of the sacred? How to effect the transformation of the ordinary? How to produce magical signs, art objects possessed of a spiritual meaning that is nevertheless not dependent on a collective religiosity and operates autonomously of the vocabulary and understanding of organised religion?

Or, posed from another angle: how can the artist restore magic to modern pictorial signs, present them as resources, or at the very least as indices, of hope and faith in a time when the centrality of *dharma* has receded in favour of other modes of self-regulation, self-inquiry, self-examination, and so of navigation through life. And in this debate, a context of comparison and association with Western art becomes inevitable, for we see a confluence, a *saṅgama* of art histories here.

From this point onwards, I will simply employ the personal voice, the first person; for the history of exploration that I am about to delineate is one in which I have invested my own emotions, as a writer who shares intimately in the dilemmas, the struggles, the surprises and the pleasures of post-colonial Indian art.

V. Abstraction and Spirituality: On the Way Home?

An encounter with an isolated painting by Mark Rothko, typically hung in a museum among works by his fellow Abstract Expressionists, can burn itself into the viewer's consciousness. And though I had already received this rite of baptism, it had not prepared me for the conversion experience I underwent at the Tate in the summer of 1996. Stepping into the special Rothko exhibition was like stepping into a cathedral; in the deliberately dimmed light, the paintings loomed like altarpieces, magisterial compositions that commanded an almost automatic reverence.

Their austere rectangular forms came through in subtle yet lavish colours, laid over one another in veils: sombre reds, glowing maroons, slow-burning blacks and luminous umbers. In that tenebrous chamber, the paintings seemed like the testaments of a prophet leading an errant tribe, tablets of revelation wrought from fire and darkness.

Rothko himself had never been in any doubt about the nature of his art. In a 1943 radio broadcast, also published as a letter to the New York Times, he and Adolph Gottlieb announced the tenets of the movement that has since come to be called Abstract Expressionism: the primacy of eternal symbols and the belief in the expressive power of myth; the modern artist's kinship with primitive man; the performance of art as a ritual, an invocation addressed to the numen, the unknown and unknowable presence dwelling within the universe.

The Tate exhibition reinforced these values: the curators had provided the art-works with an appropriate ritual context, displaying them in a manner that accentuated and affirmed their aura, their reverberant sense of having renounced the trivia of everyday life in favour of the transcendent. For the particular strain of romanticism that runs through the art of Rothko and his contemporaries, Jackson Pollock, Barnett Newman, Clyfford Still and Robert Motherwell, aspires to nothing less than the heroic, monumental defiance of history by the individual artist: the abolition of the representational particular in the name of the sublime.

Insistent as they were on the importance of the spiritual quest "in a time without a legend or mythos" (as Newman put it, in 1948), these mid-century American painters seemed to have fulfilled the prophecy that Wassily Kandinsky had made over three decades earlier. In the Introduction to his Concerning the Spiritual in Art (1912), one of the seminal manifestos of modern art, Kandinsky had suggested that the artist's soul would emerge, "refined by struggle and suffering" from a long period of "materialist temptation".

Setting his prognosis for art within this Theosophical scheme, Kandinsky continued:

> Cruder emotions, like fear, joy and grief, which belonged to this time of trial, will no longer attract the artist. He will attempt to arouse more refined emotions, as yet unnamed. Just as he will live a complicated and subtle life, so his work will give to those observers capable of feeling them emotions subtle beyond words.

The Abstract Expressionists had certainly suffered tribulation: World War II had thrown up a new and disturbing moral landscape, its sources of fertility hidden beneath the debris of trauma. Not surprisingly, the situation had militated against, rather than towards, the spiritual awakening of which Kandinsky dreamt. Children of their epoch, many of them Jewish, Rothko and his confreres were more inclined towards a tragic rather than an optimistic view of existence; but they shared Kandinsky's conviction that the artist was a pioneer of uncharted psychological regions. In their interpretation, the priestly visionary became a hero struggling with solitude, silence and mortality, earning the privilege of mystical ecstasy through the hard, stoic work of pushing the self to the extremes.

This is a self-image to which many Indian artists would relate; it confirms the persistence of the past even in the most ironic and aggressively contemporary art practices. Abstract Expressionism remains a pivotal moment in the history of modern art, precisely because it codifies so many paradoxical continuities: self-consciously American as it was, the movement restated a prophetic vision that had emerged from Asia to dazzle Europe; metropolitan in location, it drew inspiration from a romantic tribal anthropology. Above all, it placed art at the service of epiphany, defying the age of mechanical reproduction to create a High Modernism that freely acknowledged the religious impulse in art, the experience of wonder and terror that seizes the viewer in the presence of the sublime.

These are themes that lie at the core of the Indian consciousness; it is intriguing that the Abstract Expressionists should have wrestled with them in the same decade that post-colonial Indian art was born. The sublime, in all its bewildering nuances, has never been remote from the epic text, the painted surface, the sculpted volume in India. The sensation of awe, the recognition of the miraculous, the thrill of the enigmatic and the grotesque: these are heirlooms that the classical and folk traditions have bequeathed upon modern Indian art, inscribed into its charter from the beginning. The generalisation stands, irrespective of whether that beginning is located in the work of Raja Ravi Varma, Rabindranath Tagore, Amrita Sher-Gil or the Progressive Artists Group of Bombay: all these alternative founder figures gathered impetus, in some measure, from the ancestral magic.

The most programmatic, if not necessarily the most compelling project aimed at the attainment of the spiritual in art was neo-Tāntrism, an umbrella grouping that includes artists like Biren De, Ghulam Rasool Santosh, S. H. Raza, K. C. S. Paniker, Prafulla Mohanti and Akkitham Narayanan. The label is not one with which many of these artists are comfortable, nor should it be taken to mean a collective project; it merely points to the general origin of their images in the symbolic vocabulary employed during the ritual elaborations of the Tantrayāna cults.

The neo-Tantrism did not reproduce the sacred diagrams of these heterodox seekers, so much as they adopted their key motifs as points of departure. Embodying as they do the Tantrayāna ideal of the marriage of opposite principles, these motifs enshrine the possibility of communion between mind and body, human consciousness and nature, motive energy and sustaining field, the masculine and the feminine.

VI. Parallel Realities: Between Sentiment and Discipline

The desire to dissolve all dualities has always characterised Indian religious thought, but where the Vedāntic tradition would phrase it in the rarefied terminology of self and Overself, the Tantrayāna tradition dramatises it vividly, using the metaphor of carnal love to signal the overcoming of individual boundaries, the absorption of self and other in a wholeness. It is possible to deduce, from the ascendancy that neo-Tāntricism once enjoyed, that it permitted some Indian painters to exteriorise psychological conflicts that they had not been able to voice in a social environment that was shaped by an oppressive combination of feudal patriarchalism and Victorian morality.

While engendering an emotional liberation of the kind outlined above, neo-Tāntrism also secured for its practitioners an emancipation from the post-colonial ideology of social and national concern, and the leaden pictorial baggage this entailed. In the festival of choices so inaugurated, artists could abandon themselves to the exuberant play of calligraphic forms ranging from graffiti-like markings through quasi-scientific formulaic notations to impromptu hieroglyphics; or they could intoxicate themselves with the enchantment of colour reprieved from the mandate of objective, representational meaning.

These painterly manoeuvres give rise to a question of formal and semantic orientation. To the Tantrayāna adept, the painting is only a means: it has no purpose beyond the ceremonial economy in which it plays a role as vehicle of sacred energies. In the neo-Tāntrist's hands, however, the painting becomes an end in itself: it concedes its origins, but asserts itself as an autonomous sign in a semiotic economy. Several implications follow from this difference. First, though neo-Tāntricism employs a coded symbolic language drawn from traditional sources, it is a modern idiom. Second, it is a secular, not a sacred code: since it does not reflect momentous cosmic events so much as it conveys the freight of events taking place within the artist's consciousness, its meaning is private and allusive rather than secret and esoteric. In the circumstances, although the neo-Tāntricist vocabulary is to an extent shared by artist and viewer, its syntax is an idiosyncratic one; and so, the semantic contract between artist and viewer breaks down, as it has done in much contemporary art.

The advantage of this breakdown is that neo-Tāntrism may then produce a lyrical beauty that invites full-bodied responses which are not constrained by the pressure of the self-consciously spiritual (often Raza, Mohanti). The peril, however, is that many neo-Tantricists have been tempted into the default position of atavism, falling back on an iconography that no longer carries the charge it once did (often Santosh, Narayanan). When the motif is clung to for its residual significance, it cannot evolve into an image. It lingers in the province of the decorative, a victim of what might be designated the Mondrian syndrome: at a certain point of over-refinement, when monotony of content overrules diversity of form, the motif loses its unique vigour and achieves a complacent popularity instead, being replicated across a range of products including shower curtains, bags and rugs.

It may be argued that creativity orientates itself through a judicious combination of two modes: self-indulgent sentiment and self-critical discipline. The flaccidity of many neo-Tāntricist paintings may be attributed to an excess of sentiment; and those artists who wish to approach the spiritual in art by other means have learned to value discipline. They have refined for themselves a number of contemplative idioms along the spectrum between symbolism and abstractionism.

In their various ways, J. Swaminathan, V. S. Gaitonde, Nasreen Mohamedi, Ram Kumar, Jehangir Sabavala, Akbar Padamsee, Laxman Shreshtha, Prabhakar Kolte, Mehlli Gobhai, Shambhavi and Chittrovanu Mazumdar have accepted the challenge of operating among the ruins of a culture. They apprehend the phenomenal world and the forces that lie beyond its horizons as manifested in a Rilkean energy: this is not overtly cadenced in terms of the spiritual and their images are not, therefore, mediated through a specific religious iconography.

These painters begin with the stimulating awareness that the continuities of tradition have been ruptured; that artistic production now invariably takes the shape of the fragment, the clue, the hymn sung in distress. Gaitonde, Swaminathan and Kolte record, in varying degrees of excitement, the hieroglyphic annunciations of nature, the subtle translation of the primitive into the iconic. Gobhai's paintings are layered over and incised until they resemble geological archives, talismans against decay.

In the effulgent canvasses of Ram Kumar, Jehangir Sabavala, Akbar Padamsee and Laxman Shreshtha, landscape is concentrated to a point of intensity at which the chaotic local particulars of place are transfigured into a parallel reality. Shambhavi's deep saturations of colour are an invitation to the trance; Chittrovanu Mazumdar's constructions hold memories of absent icons; and Nasreen Mohamedi's ascetic, delicately minimalist works pursue the trajectories of monochromatic lines and curves that resonate in empty pictorial space.

Geometry and sensuality are held in meditative counterpoint in the works of these artists; a visceral sensation of time's processes washes against the serenity of the arrested moment; the negotiation of turbulent colour and texture leads us towards the decipherment of radiance. These paintings and constructions are oblique approaches; the artist, in each case, is not paralysed by the transcendental mystery s/he confronts, but is transported by the delight of achieving dialogue with the universe.

VII. In the Presence of the Numinous

The symbolists and abstractionists whose concerns we have just glimpsed are united in their perception of the numinous as the means by which we pass from anguish to freedom, crisis to grace - if only in that brief interval of rapture during which, as Ibn Khaldun suggests, the human soul is exalted, and returns to earth "after having received, in the world of angels, a message which it has to carry to its own kind." But the rapture of the numinous is possible only through encounter with an art-work whose aura emanates, not from high-mindedness of content, but from a mercurial, ever-renewed felicity of form; these artists know that presence cannot be apprehended except through materiality; that it is, ironically, the sensuous appeal of embodiment which maintains the integrity and potency of the numinous.

Only by shifting the emphasis from content to form can we understand how our sensibility summons forth an aura, an answering energy from art-works of the kind we have been discussing here. The object of our attention changes as we watch it, even though the physical conditions have not perceptibly been altered; the phenomenon recalls to mind the thermodynamic concept of latent heat, the heat radiated by a substance during a change of phase at constant temperature and pressure.

This transitive conception of the aura, the latent heat of the art-work, is one way of responding to the debate over the spirit-form relationship that has long exercised Indian aesthetic theory. In the 20th century, this debate has been dominated by the influential but constricting views of Ananda Coomaraswamy. Speaking from the classical position of Ṣanskrit aesthetics, the great savant treated sensuous form as a mere prelude to, or at best a vehicle for grand spiritual abstractions. It seems to me that this Idealist rhetoric fails to grasp the fundamental importance of the symbiosis between pneuma and morphe, presence and materiality: it is this creative dialectic which accounts for the real power of the spiritual in art.

We have, so far, considered only the abstractionist and the symbolist approaches to the spiritual in art. But there is also the terrain between this classical-sublime and the romantic-picturesque associated with that flourishing firm, Ravi Varma & Co., painters extraordinary to the courts, oleographers to the public, illustrators of religious subjects in whose works the Hindu deities and heroes were choreographed by Alma-Tadema and the Pre-Raphaelites.

In this intermediate terrain between Ravi Varma and Rothko, a delightful variety of narrative and figurative accounts lay claim upon the imagination, and a carnival of images unfolds. It is grim and lively by turns, and the mythology is the message. But since this is a period that lacks clear and present sources of authority, new iconographies must be invented: this procedure allows, fortunately, for rupture and renewal, the coding of the individual obsession into the collective mythology.

Such a quest for an irrefutably convincing centre of vitality, as against the worship of a fossil motif, yields Tyeb Mehta's fierce Kālī and Mahiṣāsura-mardinī, Manjit Bawa's rhapsodic Krishna and Shiva, Arpita Singh's Devi armed with the weaponry of the present, Mrinalini Mukherjee's stately rope sculptures of *yakṣīs*, Badri Narayan's allegories of monks and nymphs in modern suburbia, Rekha Rodwittiya's goddesses of grace and abundance, N Rimzon's solitary *tīrthaṅkara* maintaining his poise while standing at the centre of a circle of swords.

The playfulness of the pastorale and the solemnity of the sacrifice are equally valid registers of the numinous in this zone; miniatures from royal ateliers, bazaar prints, folk theatre and votive sculpture are all treated as resources to be recycled, and the storyteller begins to vein the numinous with colloquial asides. Buoyant as they are, these images remind us that the spiritual in art is not a territory defined by maps. It is a space that is intimate and yet resonant with cosmic overtures, a space in which we can, like the Polish poet Miron Bialoszewski, cry out: "Higher/ clarion calls of form,/ habitations of touch,/ all serenities of the senses.../ Strike me/ construction of my world!"

ENDNOTES

1. The Loom of Time. Penguin. 1968
2. Chāndogya Upaniṣad. 8.1.3 and 8.15.1

6

The Dead and the Dying: Post Modern Reactions to the Despair of Modernity

Harsha V. Dehejia

If modernity in India* had its unique hues and texture post-modernism evolved equally distinctively and it has been rightly said that both modernity and post-modernism develop in a particular socio-cultural situation. It can also be said that Western models are not always useful to reflect Indian realities. Engaging in a discourse on post-modernity is somewhat like putting up a scaffolding to inspect a dilapidated *havelī* and then finding that the scaffolding itself is unstable, for one of the features of postmodernity is the crisis of all semiotic and structural analysis, disabling and paralyzing any attempt to move from an outer world of chaos to an inner world of order. Postmodernity is not only de-centered but de-centering, centrifugal rather than centripetal, defying any attempt to contain it in an ordered space, and therefore in the end it deludes the dialectic of meaning. Our interest in looking at post-modernity in India is a limited one, and that is to find out whether or not the emotion of despair, which we have postulated as the defining emotion of modernity for us in Indian painting, still persists in the mind of the urban intellectual artist in the post-modern period.

Strictly speaking post-modernism, which is perhaps a reaction

---

* I acknowledge with gratitude the many discussions I have had with Ranjit Hoskote on this subject and for letting me borrow substantially from his essay Art: From Enchantment to Interrogation in Independent India, The First Fifty Years. Indian Council for Cultural Relations. Delhi. Oxford University Press. 1998

to modernity, should not be considered as a resolution to modernity. The language of discourse of post-modernism is the same as that of modernity but the texture is different. Post-modernism is an outgrowth and not a corrective to modernity. But inasmuch as it arises along side modernity, it is important that we conclude our inquiry by looking briefly at post-modernity in the context of despair in modern India.

It was in 1985 that Amitabha Gupta first used the term *uttara ādhunikatā* in the journal Janapada. Some have defined post-modernism as modernity with a historical recall. This definition stresses the nostalgic aspect of post-modernism which for us in India is not as pertinent as it is in the West, as the past in India is always a part of the present. Others define post-modernism as a state of overlapping images and ideas, with a loss of definition at the edges, as in a collage or montage. Yet others define post-modernism as the collapse of meaning. Despite the rhetoric of rebellion post-modernism is to be regarded as an extension of the modern civilizing process. Whichever definition one accepts a basic feature of post-modernism is the coming together of two contrasting, but not necessarily opposing, images and ideas, one delegitimising the other. Post-modernism brings together the ancient with the modern, the folk and the classical, the profound with the banal, the celestial with the earthly, the hieratic with demonic, the religious with the secular and the ascetic with the voluptuous. There is thus in post-modern images a certain playfulness, a sense of airiness, a loss of structure, a blending of realities, a fusion of the real with the surreal. In keeping away from any rigid discourse or ideology, post-modernism creates a softer, less strident ambience. There is none of the hard rationality of modernity, the refined grace of the classical, the ordered universe of the Purāṇas or the charged emotions of the romantic *rasakāvyas.* Instead there is in post-modern images the beauty and celebration of banality. Equally there is in the Indian post-modern psyche an acceptance that the rigidity of rationality and the aridity of despair must not allow the mind to be deprived of its innate freedom to roam in vast and unbounded spaces. There is thus in post-modern vistas a desire to transcend the restricted spaces of modernity, a desire on the one hand to accept the inevitability of modernity but at the same time to reach out and touch a certain sportive, playful, almost child like side of the human condition.

There are two groups of artists who should be considered in the group of post-modern image makers for us in India. There are those who have experienced and expressed modernity through images of despair, but have mellowed in their twilight years to express themselves through the softer and airy images of post-modernity. And then there are the younger artists who may or may not have had a brush with modernity, but who were indeed exposed to the images of despair created by the older generation of artists, but who preferred to launch directly into post-modern imagery without expressing the initial despair of modernity.

If modernity, while breaking away from tradition, sets up its own unique discourse, post-modernists prefer to stay at the margins and avoid entering into any rigid and didactic discourse. Post-modernists uphold ideas and images of those who are at the fringes of society, whose voices were either too unimportant or too feeble to be heard in the main stream of society. These would include the voices and concerns of the minorities, the downtrodden, the deviant. Unlike various post-modern social movements, or post-modern literature that seek to correct past wrongs, post-modern images tend to be less strident. They suggest rather than advocate, whisper rather than shout and draw the onlooker gently into their message.

One of the ways it which it achieves this is by setting up small narratives or little myths which do not have the grandeur or vastness of our ancient *purāṇas*, but all the same tell a story or recreate an event in their own terms. The small narratives of post-modern images lack both myth and fantasy and unlike ancient myths have no ontologic or epsitemological intentions. Myth without ontology and narrative without epistemology remains necessarily playful and sportive. In the ethos of post-modernism received mythologies can be interrogated and disputed while new and contemporary mythologies may be brought into being. Steering away from didactic images of yore these playful post-modern images reinvent enchantment and reintroduce wonder, both of which were lost in the arid and fragmented images of despair of modernity. *Adbhuta* or wonder that is such an important part of the human psyche and a pre-requisite for transcendence, and which was lost in the aridity of rationality, is felt and expressed again by post-moderns in their unique way. The emotion of wonder that is so integral to a child-like appraisal of the world and which is equally a pre-requisite for transcendent *ānanda*, is felt and expressed by our post-modern artists. When the dead weight of unbridled rationality is removed, the mind's innate ability to rejoice and celebrate, to feel the joy and the splendor of the human condition, to engage once again in mythopoesis albeit of the little variety, is allowed to flourish. However unlike the classical traditions post-modern thinking and images tend to be open ended, they are centrifugal rather than centripetal and lead the mind not into a central *bindu* of energy and rest but into an amorphous and joyous state of a centripetal carnival. The ethos of post-modern images is therefore playful without being childish, airy without being frivolous, discursive without being didactic, folkish rather than elitist, and celebrate uncertainties without imposing any established verities. It is the genius of post-modernism to tackle the nature of uncertainties with forms that exist without a rigid structure or organized space. Post-modern image makers recover the process of play or *līlā* and make it a serious principle of construction, operation and effect. Through play they create a space in which argument and theatre, ritual and circus can all take place simultaneously.

These features of post-modern images are perhaps best seen in installations rather than in images on canvas. Installations tend to blur the boundary between the gallery and the world and gently, almost subversively, draw the onlooker into it as they yoke aesthetic desire to political agency, pleasure to labor, the carnival to the machine. Installations highlight the process as much as the end product and emphasize the art of making. By privileging the quirky and the visceral meaning over the abstract and the transcendental, the artwork becomes an object of aesthetic encounter that supplies the viewer with a strategy for its own reading even as it is being read. It acts often as a koan, a riddle, a ruse: a trope of impossibility that gives material embodiment to the vexing yet replenishing conditions of paradox. What results from these manouvers is the informalization, the democratization, the desacralization of the image.

With the collapse of meaning post-modern images exist in a space of quietened, if not deadened, emotions, a non-space, a semiotic black hole, a space where discourse has been seduced and where structure has crumbled and any attemp at analysis is only met by a mocking silence; it is a space of simulations and simulacra, a space where there is of lack of certainties and instead a celebration of instability; it is a space of infinite implosion into which all meaning is absorbed. While despair characterized some of our modern images, yet they were images born out of a certain emotive reaction, for despair is also a human emotion. In post-modernism on the other hand the collapse of meaning, for both the artist and the aesthete, creates a state of paralysis of emotion. While post-modern images are animated, the level of emotion is flattened or muted. In particular the strident depiction of despair is certainly not a feature of these images.

If the classical and medieval period of India's artistic tradition was characterized by a celebration and realisation of eight and then later ten *rasas,* and if modernity for us in India was defined by the new emotion of despair, the post-modern period is marked by a collapse, a flattening, a deflation, a deadening of emotion. Traditional aesthetic doctrines maintain *pratīti eva rasanā, rasa* is a special type of knowing, where the artist and the aesthete alike taste *rasa* and in its realization find aesthetic bliss. This is the bliss of knowledge, a transcendent joy of perfect stillness, the wonder of an aesthetic experience that has been brought to its fruition and end point. We have argued that even despair is a *rasa* in its own right, for the realisation of despair through its artistic manifestations has led to knowledge. However the flattened affect of post-modern images does not lend itself to an emotional probe, it is animation without a strident emotion, it is an art object without a defining *rasa* It is emotional indifference, a smiling face smiling at nothing in particular. Rukmini

Bhaya Nair[1] locates this indifference in the post-colonial malaise; equally the post-modern state arises from the catharsis of urban intellectual despair.

If one were to pick one image out of many that illustrates this non-*rasa* of post-modernity it would be the Dead and Dying by Krishan Khanna. Underneath a cadaver three people play cards. While two police officers point to the dead body, the three totally unaffected, non-chalant, self-absorbed and self-assured in their ennui play a game of cards. There is neither grief nor excitement in their faces, just the satisfaction that their time is being well spent in pondering their next move in the game of cards, oblivious of the state of the world, disinterested and unable to undertake weighty issues, unconcerned that a life has just ended and that their's might be next. The beauty in this image is that of banality, of body and mind, while the unknown cadaver rests in its final dignity.

ENDNOTS

1. Rukmini Bhaya Nair. Postcoloniality and the Matrix of Indifference. pp 7-24. India International Quarterly. Summer 1999.

ABOUT THE AUTHORS

Harsha V. Dehejia has a double doctorate, one in Medicine and the other in Ancient Indian Culture, both from the University of Mumbai. He is also a Fellow of the Royal College of Physicians of London, Glasgow and Canada, all by examination. He is Professor of Religion at Carleton University in Ottawa, Canada where he teaches Indian Aesthetics. He has published three books, *The Advaita of Art, Pārvatīdarpana* (both by Motilal Banarasidass, Delhi) and *Pārvati, Goddess of Love* (by Mapin, Ahmedabad). He is Curatorial Advisor to the Canadian Museum of Civilization. Dr. Dehejia is a practicing physician and lives in Ottawa.

Prem Shankar Jha, studied at the Doon School, St. Stephen College, Delhi and Magdalen College, Oxford. He holds a B.A. in Economics and an M.A. in Philosophy, Politics and Economics. After five years in the United Nations Development Programme in New York and Damascus he returned to India in 1966 to become a journalist. In the past thirty years, he has been Economic Editor of The Times of India, Editor of The Economic Times and Financial Express and finally editor of The Hindustan Times. From 1986 to 1990 he was the India correspondent of The Economist, London. In 1990 he was Information Advisor to Prime Minister V.P. Singh. At present, he is a columnist for the The Business Standard and The Hindu and writes in several other papers both in India and abroad. He has been a visiting fellow of Nuffield College, Oxford and Center for International Affairs, Harvard University, Cambridge and a visiting Professor at the University of Virginia. Mr. Jha is the author of four books: *India, A Political Economy Of Stagnation, Management Of The Public Sector In Developing Asian Countries*: a handbook, *In The Eye Of The Cyclone: The Crisis of Indian Democracy and Kashmir: Rival Versions Of History.* At present, Mr. Jha is working on a book on The Impact Of

Globalization On International Peace. A book on the capitalist transformation in India, China and Russia is currently under publication. Mr. Jha has written extensively on Indian classical music and dance and is the co-founder of Baithak, a society devoted to the promotion of Indian music in intimate settings.

Ranjit Hoskote, is a poet, art critic and translator. In 1995, Hoskote was Visiting Writer of the International Writing Program at the University of Iowa, U.S.A. His publications include *Zones Of Assault* (1991) (tr), *A Terrorist Of The Spirit* (1992), *Pilgrim, Exile, Sorcerer:The Painterly Evolution Of Jehangir Sabavala* (1998). His poems have appeared in anthologies and various journals, including The Poetry Review, The Lines Review and The Indian PEN Quarterly. Mr.Hoskote won the Sanskriti Award for Literature in 1996 and the British Council Poetry Society prize in 1997.

Ashis Nandy trained as a sociologist and clinical psychologist. Nandy's research interests are political psychology, culture of knowledge, utopias and visions, popular culture and futures. He is presently Senior Fellow of the Centre for the Study of Developing Societies and the Chairperson of the Committee for Cultural Choices and Global Futures, both at Delhi.

Preciously, he has been Director of the Centre for the Study of Developing Societies (1992-1997); Woodrow Wilson Fellow, Woodrow Wilson International Center, Washington (1988); Charles Wallace Fellow, Department of Politics, The University of Hull (1990); Fellow, Institute for Advanced Studies in Humanities, The University of Edinburgh (1991);UNESCO Professor, Centre for European Studies, University of Trier, Germany (1994); and Regent's Fellow, University of California, Los Angeles.

Among Nandy's books are: *Alternative Sciences* (1980,1995); *At The Edge of Psychology* (1980); *The Intimate Enemy* (1983); *Traditions, Tyranny and Utopias* (1987); *The Tao of Cricket* (1989); *The Illegitimacy of Nationalism* (1994); *The Savage Freud and Other Essays in Possible and Retrievable Selves* (1995); He is also a co-author of *The Blinded Eye* (1993) also published as *Barbaric Others*; and *Creating a Nationality* (1995). Nandy has edited two books: *Science, Hegemony and Violence* (1988) and *The Secret Politics of our Desires* (forthcoming); and co-edited *The Multivlerse of Democracy* (1996). Oxford University Press is now bringing out an omnibus edition of all his works. Nandy's works have been translated into a number of languages, among them Bengali, Chinese, Finnish, French, German, Hindi, Italian, Japanese, Malayalam, Marathi, Polish, Russian, Spanish and Tamil. He has also contributed to major human rights reports on ethnic and communal violence and democratic elections.